WHAT WORKS?

OTHER TITLES FROM BLOOMSBURY EDUCATION

Bloomsbury CPD Library: Research-Informed Practice, by Jennifer Ludgate

Celebrating Difference, by Shaun Dellenty

Education: A Manifesto for Change, by Richard Gerver

Just Great Teaching, by Ross Morrison McGill

The Arts in Primary Education, by Ghislaine Kenyon

The Wellbeing Toolkit, by Andrew Cowley

WHAT WORKS?

Research and evidence for successful teaching

Lee Elliot Major and Steve Higgins

BLOOMSBURY EDUCATION

LONDON OXFORD NEW YORK NEW DELHI SYDNEY

BLOOMSBURY EDUCATION
Bloomsbury Publishing Plc
50 Bedford Square, London, WC1B 3DP, UK

BLOOMSBURY, BLOOMSBURY EDUCATION and the Diana logo
are trademarks of Bloomsbury Publishing Plc

First published in the UK by Bloomsbury Education

A catalogue record for this book is available from the British Library

ISBN: PB: 978-1-4729-6563-9; ePDF: 978-1-4729-6562-2;
ePub: 978-1-4729-6561-5

2 4 6 8 10 9 7 5 3

Text design by Marcus Duck Design
Typeset by Newgen KnowledgeWorks Pvt. Ltd., Chennai, India
Printed and bound in the UK by CPI Group (UK) Ltd, Croydon, CR0 4YY

To find out more about our authors and books visit www.bloomsbury.com
and sign up for our newsletters

CONTENTS

INTRODUCTION: BANANARAMA AND BEST BETS FOR LEARNING

Teachers always laugh at the joke. The Bananarama Principle is named after Bananarama and Fun Boy Three's 1982 hit single 'It Ain't What You Do'. The original song 'T'aint what you do, (it's the way that cha do it)' was written by jazz musicians Melvin 'Sy' Oliver and James 'Trummy' Young in 1939, and was made famous by Ella Fitzgerald and the 'Shim Sham' tap dance routine. And it's essential advice for today's educators acting on the findings of research. For many teachers the 1980s cultural reference conjures up a bygone era. But the catchy ska riff sticks in their minds. It's the most important thing we have to say.

This guiding law came to life in 2011 when we toured the country to share with teachers the Pupil Premium Toolkit (Higgins et al., 2011). Published by the Sutton Trust charity, the toolkit offered an accessible *Which*-style guide detailing best bets for improving children's attainment. The UK Coalition Government had ring-fenced Pupil Premium funds for schools to help improve the results of their poorest pupils, who continued to lag behind their more privileged peers (Department for Education, 2010a). Our point was a simple one: it wouldn't be what schools spent, but the way they spent it that would get results.

The Pupil Premium Toolkit was born from a meeting of two different minds – a product of compromise. That's its strength and its weakness. One of us (Steve) was obsessed with making meta-synthesis – the summarising of thousands of studies – a practical tool for teachers (Higgins, 2018). This guide would provide the big-picture view, hovering above the research landscape and rising above the contradictory and conflicting conclusions from single studies. And one of us (Lee) was convinced we should spend as much time translating the complex jargon of academe into an accessible language for teachers as producing the findings in the first place. Research summaries had existed before. But like so many publications, they were soon gathering dust on long-forgotten library shelves.

Combining these goals was a balancing act. Syntheses of research are only as good as the assumptions they're built on and the quality of studies they summarise. If you simplify the messages too much, the true story gets lost in crude headlines. The first toolkit (Higgins et al., 2011) was a 20-page report collating findings from thousands of studies corralled into evidence summaries for 20 teaching approaches aimed at improving learning.

A lot of thinking went into the design and presentation of the guide. It presented the costs of implementing the approaches and the strength of evidence underpinning our conclusions of how well it had worked. Brave calls were made translating effect sizes, the comparative impacts of interventions, from the language of statistics into a more meaningful measure for everyday classroom use: extra months gained during an academic year (the assumptions we made in order to do this are explained in the technical notes on page xxii). These estimates are less precise than the underlying statistics, but they are realistic guides, given the limitations of the research findings on which they stand.

Without this, the toolkit wouldn't have caught the imagination of busy classroom professionals. Teachers immediately got it.

Our toolkit talks made for lively debates. They were attended by thousands of teachers and senior school leaders across the country. This too was a respectful coming together of two different perspectives. The best discussion came when the findings gathered by academics under idealised conditions collided with the practical everyday realities of teachers' working lives. Together we would tease out how the big-picture lessons applied on ground level.

The counter-intuitive conclusions caused a stir (Major, 2012). On a grey last day of term in Cambridgeshire we unveiled to hundreds of teaching assistants (TAs) the humbling finding that assistants, on average, added little to pupil achievement. It was a difficult meeting. No caveats or constructive comments could calm the enraged ranks of TAs. All they could see was an attack on their livelihoods. Below this average finding lay the real story. TAs properly managed, prepared and trained, and working alongside teachers, had significant impact on children; those without support, and allocated pupils with severe learning needs, struggled. In other words, it wasn't deploying teaching assistants or not that mattered most, but how they were deployed.

Reducing class sizes had surprisingly limited impact on pupil progress. Smaller classes are a school priority promoted by politicians, parents and teachers alike. But studies have found the benefits of reducing class sizes are not large or clear, until class size is reduced to under 20 or as low as 15 pupils per teacher. Teachers bridled at this conclusion. Many argued smaller classes were effective when serving children with special educational needs or challenging behaviour. The devil was in the research details. Smaller classes work when teachers change the way they teach, catering to individual needs of pupils and receiving more feedback from children on what they need to learn next. It's not reducing class size that matters, but how you adapt your teaching style with fewer pupils.

Grouping children by 'ability' as ever split opinions. For every passionate believer in mixed-ability teaching, there was an equally convinced advocate of academic setting. Evidence accumulated over several decades could not settle these apparently irreconcilable views. The reason was buried in the finer details of the toolkit: the quality of teaching trumps how children are organised. Delivered poorly, neither mixed-ability classes nor sets work; delivered well, both can be effective.

The use of teaching assistants, reducing class sizes and ability grouping are all examples of the Bananarama Principle. The Principle underscores the power but also limitations of evidence in helping a teacher decide what to do in a classroom: how an approach is implemented is vital and just as important as its content. Evidence is necessary, but never sufficient.

Success – a doubled-edged sword

The Pupil Premium Toolkit revealed an insatiable appetite for evidence. Adopted by the Education Endowment Foundation (EEF), it became the *Sutton Trust-EEF Teaching and Learning Toolkit*. When launched by the Government in 2010, the EEF, funded with an initial £110-million endowment was compared to the 'Race to the Top' competition in the United States (Department for Education, 2010b). In reality the EEF did something different: promoting the use of evidence in schools and funding randomised trials assessing the effectiveness of different approaches and programmes in English schools. The EEF nurtured and developed the toolkit into the 35-strand interactive website you see today at: https://educationendowmentfoundation.org.uk/evidence-summaries/teaching-learning-toolkit. When the school inspectorate in England, Ofsted, gave it a seal of approval, it turned overnight into a must-read for headteachers, who had to report back on how they were using their Pupil Premium funds.

By 2015 two-thirds of school leaders across England reported they had used the toolkit (Cockburn et al., 2015). Versions have been launched in Scotland (https://education.gov.scot/improvement/eefsearch), Australia (https://evidenceforlearning.org.au/the-toolkit), Spain (www.educaixa.com/es/listado-evidencias) and Latin America (www.summaedu.org/plataforma-de-practicas-educativas-efectivas), with other countries waiting in the wings. It has helped to create a more evidence-informed culture in classrooms across the world. Teachers ask questions about research in a way they didn't a decade ago. Hardly a day goes by when one of us doesn't meet a teacher who excitedly encourages us to look at the toolkit they have discovered – not knowing we are its creators!

But the problem with popularity is you lose sight of the reasons that made you successful in the first place. The toolkit's findings were digested directly without the nuances, caveats and ambiguities that can be explained during face-to-face discussion. Research claims were treated as unassailable truths. Classrooms were assumed to be the same homogenous units. Best bets turned into absolute certainties.

The UK Government cited the toolkit as an exemplar for its new network of 'What Works' centres – for policing, early interventions, ageing – alongside those already established for health and education (Cabinet Office, 2013). This drive to spend public money on the most effective practices was laudable, but the 'What Works' label can imply a certainty that oversimplifies reality. Research can only tell us what has worked in the past, not what will work in the future. Indeed, it can only offer indications of what may work under certain conditions.

The toolkit's findings were presented by some journalists as stark, black-and-white decisions. 'Setting and streaming? NO. Teaching assistants? NO,' declared a BBC journalist briefed to write about the Government's new initiative (Easton, 2014). The complexities of converting research into practice had been bastardised into a binary code. Research headlines prompted knee-jerk reactions. We made the case for training teaching assistants – and the teachers working with them – not sacking them.

Meanwhile parallels were made with the movement to create more evidence-based practice in medicine (see www.nice.org.uk). There are several reasons why the pharmaceutical model of research doesn't apply in education, not least of which is that it isn't clear who is supposed to take the tablets in a classroom. The 'medicine' has to be palatable to the teacher yet effective with the pupils. A classroom is a much more complex place than a consulting room. You usually have one teacher and 30 pupils. It is like finding the prescription to make all your patients healthy, when they are suffering from a range of undiagnosed medical conditions.

It was only a matter of time for a backlash to this drive to make teaching an evidence-led profession to erupt. Prominent education figures argued we were deluded to think teaching could ever be completely research-based (Wiliam, 2015). Others said it was compromising the freedom of teachers to decide what's best to do for the unique make-up of children in their classrooms. Some argued evidence couldn't answer education's most important question: what is it for? (Biesta, 2007)

Surveys of teachers meanwhile revealed greater recognition of evidence, but scant signs of more focus on the approaches shown by the toolkit to offer the highest chance of improving attainment (Sutton Trust, 2013). Only one in 25 teachers had prioritised improving feedback between teachers and pupils, an inexpensive measure with the potential to add eight months to pupils' learning in one year. And only one in 100 said they would use peer-to-peer tutoring schemes, another highly promising approach according to the toolkit.

Publishing the evidence doesn't automatically lead to schools adapting their teaching practices. And some teachers got it plain wrong. We were concerned to hear stories of schools devoting extra hours to the marking of pupils' work under the false belief this would deliver effective feedback. One local authority in Scotland tried to use the toolkit as justification for *increasing* class sizes, failing to consider the overall evidence that pupils in larger classes tend to do a little bit less well, on average. Our argument was that reducing class sizes is only moderately effective and very expensive, so not cost-effective as a strategy to help learners.

England's trials

The inherent uncertainties of applying evidence in the classroom have been confirmed by randomised controlled trials investigating interventions in England's schools. In seven years, the EEF signed up more than 10,000 schools, nurseries and colleges to 150 randomised trials, involving one million children. Most approaches trialled are little better than 'teaching as usual' in other schools: only around a quarter of EEF studies show enough impact to warrant larger scale-up trials involving more schools (EEF, 2019a). The most promising programmes boost students' progress by an extra three months in a school year, yet the effect shrinks when scaled up to hundreds of schools.

Scour through the EEF's evaluation reports and a common thread emerges. Trials of peer tutoring in English schools are a case in point (EEF, 2017a). Peer tutoring, where pupils teach each other, is one of the most promising approaches according to evidence gathered for decades in schools across the world. Yet evaluations in England failed to find any attainment gains on average compared with teaching as usual. How could this be? In part, it was due to inferior past studies that had overestimated the size of effects. But a key aspect was the delivery. Some teachers felt more guidance and time was required to make tutoring work; others felt the programme was too prescriptive. It's tough to get the right balance between producing detailed instructions and allowing teachers to shape the programme for themselves. We perhaps also forgot that it matters *what* pupils teach each other. We need to get the content right as well as the pedagogy. Every classroom is a unique web of interactions between teachers and pupils. Delivery is difficult.

What works?

Our aim in this book is to capture the spirit of the toolkit and explore the reality of 'what works' in education. On the one hand, that means providing practical tips for teachers and leaders; on the other hand, it means instilling a healthy dose of scepticism for teachers when scrutinising how approaches are working in their own schools and classrooms. As we will explain below, this book allows us to venture into new ground, explaining the recurring principles that apply across many approaches and offering informed but more speculative viewpoints, considering a range of pupil outcomes. We assess the research and evidence for 21 different teaching approaches. We think that there are some broad principles which teachers and schools should bear in mind as they use evidence to help improve outcomes for learners in their care.

'What works?' is a deceptively simple question. The question mark in the book's title is important! Knowing something has worked in the past for some pupils and teachers is no guarantee in education for predicting what will happen in the future for other teachers and pupils. 'What works?' is shorthand for 'What has worked for whom under what conditions?'. Our best attempt at answering this is explaining how the Bananarama Principle applies for each approach.

The principle highlights the statistical pattern we observe in the summaries of effect sizes from different studies. The impact on children varies more within each toolkit strand than it does between strands. It's not choosing to do peer tutoring that matters but how well you do it. The spread of effects for an approach is as important as its average impact: it indicates what you should focus on, and what you should avoid, to maximise the chances of making an impact.

Feedback in the classroom, for example, when delivered well, yields on average higher learning gains compared with most interventions, but studies show some efforts at providing feedback can harm learning. The overall average suggests feedback is a good bet for teachers, but the variation in results raises the risk you could make things worse for your pupils.

Ella Fitzgerald sings, 'It ain't what you do, it's the time that you do it, that's what gets results' in her 1938 song. This is true for feedback, as the timing of the information given and received between teacher and pupil is crucial. Too early and you risk prompting the learner unnecessarily; too late and the moment has passed.

Limits of research

Teachers will always have limited research evidence to draw on. It will never answer every question. Our knowledge from meta-analysis is like a medieval map of the world, where some areas are better known, such as learning to read (Higgins, 2018). In other areas, the evidence is less secure, but still coherent, such as about collaborative learning or small-group teaching. There are also other areas that resemble mythical lands – fantasies such as learning styles or multiple intelligences.

Much of the educational territory has been explored, but more mapping is needed to increase the odds of successful educational decision-making. There are errors and gaps in what we know. Some of the underlying studies are not as robust as we'd like. Our approach assumes there is no systematic bias in different areas of research (Simpson, 2017). Where bias exists, this may distort some of our conclusions. Our picture isn't precise enough to inform practice as much as we would like, but it's the only approach we have and the best starting point to build upon.

Our compass showing the way ahead will never be perfect. Researchers have found practices observed among effective teachers had little predictive power when applied to a different group of teachers (Coe et al., 2014). Certain types of behaviour led to higher pupil gains, but there were always exceptions. The humbling conclusion is that the behaviour of effective teachers is hard to characterise; much depends on how teachers relate to their particular pupils (Brown et al., 2001). Great teachers are master orchestrators – knowing what to do when for what children. It's not what they do but how they do it that counts.

Coaxing learning amidst the complexities of human interactions feels more like navigating through choppy waters. Classroom feedback has been likened to throwing bottles into the sea – 'no one can be sure that the message they contain will one day find a receiver' (Hargreaves, 2011). In his seminal book *The Hidden Lives of Learners*, Graham Nuthall (2007) revealed the challenge every classroom teacher is up against: 70 per cent of pupils' time was spent pretending to listen; 80 per cent of the feedback pupils' received was from their fellow peers; and 80 per cent of this was wrong!

The education world is also an evolving ecosystem, where what works changes over time. We now know teaching assistants trained to provide specified support for one-to-one or small-group tutoring can boost pupils' learning by up to five extra months in an academic year. This comes from new evidence generated by several trials (Sharples et al., 2018). This territory has been mapped more accurately. Learning benefits were found across several subjects in both primary and secondary schools.

In this book, we have used the best evidence we can – over 200 summaries of 8,000 intervention studies assembled together. It is the best evidence we have at this point in time. If organisations like the EEF and the Institute for Education Sciences in the United States continue to fund evaluations, the quality of this evidence base will improve. We doubt this will make it more prescriptive for teachers. It is more likely to show how difficult it is to improve outcomes for children at scale (Lortie-Forgues and Inglis, 2019). But it may help us understand better what to do for whom and when.

Wider outcomes

Throughout the book, we also offer guidance on what has worked to improve wider outcomes for children, not just academic gains measured by test results. Teachers are interested in the wellbeing of their pupils. They hope they will develop into independent learners and confident adults, ready to work together with others on problems in the workplace, and succeed in life after school. Insights into these essential life skills are fewer and more speculative with less research to draw on (Gutman and Schoon, 2013a), but to ignore them is to deny how we as humans develop.

None of us want to crush a pupil's self-esteem and subliminally suggest no amount of effort will change their prospects. This is probably why setting children by perceived ability can damage their development, particularly when delivered in an inflexible way with little movement of pupils between groupings. Children from poorer backgrounds are most at risk as they often find themselves trapped in the lowest sets. It can lead to a declining spiral of low confidence, poor behaviour and inferior grades.

Interventions aiming to enhance social and emotional learning can improve children's relationships with others inside and outside school (EEF, 2018a). Pupils learn how to manage their emotions and become better learners. The most effective programmes are those embedded into routine classroom practices and supported by staff training. Successful strategies can improve children's attitudes and attainment. This is an important finding. Attributes such as self-control and perseverance have attracted the unfortunate moniker of 'non-cognitive skills'. This misses the point – they are as 'cognitive' as any learning skills. A teacher should be considering all these pupil attributes for any classroom approach. How learners think and feel are inseparable.

Participation in arts and sports activities has important educational value in itself. Such activities are associated with increased self-confidence and wellbeing, improved social interaction and leadership skills. They should be valued as part of the wider school curriculum, not just seen as a means of improving test scores. A broad and balanced curriculum is important both for individual children who can succeed across a wide range of outcomes, but also for wider society in terms of how we prepare our children and young people for the world outside school.

Unexpected findings

Research has a habit of confounding expectations and debunking received wisdom in the classroom. In each chapter, we present an unexpected gem for busy practitioners. These have the potential to improve learning but also reduce teacher workload.

Less is more applies to marking, for example. Our conclusion in the toolkit that feedback is crucial for learning gains inadvertently contributed to pressure on teachers to mark more. But the key to effective feedback is that it is given, received and acted upon. Mountains of marked papers make little impact without closing this loop. Teachers should focus on fundamental misunderstandings rather than waste time on careless mistakes. Grades for students can blind them to what they need to focus on next to make progress (Black and Wiliam, 1998).

Similarly, we have lots of evidence that phonics approaches are effective for children struggling to learn to read. But it is far from clear how much phonics successful novice readers require, and whether we should try a different strategy for children for whom phonics hasn't worked.

Teaching tips and leadership tips

We offer hundreds of snippets of practical advice for teachers and school leaders. These tips have been extracted from the academic literature with great care. Distilling research findings into actionable steps is tricky work. Summarising education evidence from hundreds of individual studies has been likened to picking the strawberries out of jam (Higgins and Hall, 2004). You can see they are there, but they are so boiled and crystallised by the meta-analytic jam-making process they no longer taste like strawberries. A recurring plea is that teachers assess and evaluate whatever they choose to do: setting clear goals, being clear how they aim to achieve them and knowing how they will measure success (see more about this in the afterword on page 125).

Principles

The Bananarama Principle – that implementation is as important as content – is one of three principles that recur across all teaching approaches. The Bananarama Principle, the Goldilocks Principle and the Matthew Effect are universal laws that provide a common thread when thinking about the complexities of the classroom. In some chapters we also feature other specific principles that relate to one particular approach.

The Goldilocks Principle

The Goldilocks Principle is about getting things just right – not too much, not too little. In the fairy tale, Goldilocks wants porridge that is not too hot or too cold. Teachers judge countless balancing acts during a school day. Goldilocks is Bananarama's little sister – a special case of how what you do matters in teaching.

The principle applies to feedback delivered in every lesson when encouraging pupils to take leaps in learning. Too much challenge creates a chasm the learner can't cross. Too little challenge and the learner loses an opportunity to learn something new. Judging the precise nudge to give is a highly attuned skill. It needs to be timely and specific. If learning goals are vague or ill-timed, learners lose faith. Feedback has to be just right. It has been likened to pushing a swing: it looks simple, but is a coordinated action requiring accurate timing, force and direction. Too gentle and the learner slows down; too hard and they fall off! (Higgins, 2018)

Getting it right also applies to homework. It's a risky teaching strategy at the best of times with no qualified teacher present when children are studying. Some homework is probably better than none for older learners, but too much turns children off learning. As children age they are able to cope with more. The research suggests no more than two hours of study an evening for older pupils (Cooper et al., 2006). In other countries, parents don't think schools should intrude on children's time once the school day has finished as they have other things to learn and enjoy.

The Matthew Effect

We hope disadvantaged pupils will benefit from more evidence-enriched classrooms. The achievement gap between poorer children and their better-off peers remains stark (Andrews et al., 2017). This divide can be observed in most classrooms, shaped by the different conditions experienced by children outside schools. Teachers' passion and perseverance are born from a commitment to do something about it.

It's an uphill climb as education acts as a positional good – it's not what qualifications you have that matters but how much better they are than those of other students. Schools have worked wonders to get many more children on free school meals passing national school benchmarks at age 16, but children from privileged homes have leaped further ahead (Major and Machin, 2018).

An international study found that around 60 per cent of achievement gaps at the age of 14 are already present at the start at schooling in England (Bradbury et al., 2015). The richest children are already 19 months ahead of the poorest pupils in school readiness when they enter primary school. About half the gap is linked with the 'home learning environment' – indicating how much factors outside school influence the learning of children. Achievement gaps are wide in countries with high levels of inequality outside the school gates. The education system acts as a counter-balance to the powerful forces outside driving bigger education gaps between the advantaged and disadvantaged.

The Pupil Premium policy, unveiled in 2010, was the latest in a long line of UK Government attempts to narrow the achievement gap (Major and Machin, 2018). This was a bold step, dedicating billions of pounds for the disadvantaged in England's schools. But we were concerned many priorities for funding were misguided bets for improving learning. One suggestion was schools could reduce class sizes. It sounded plausible but was unlikely to have much effect. The first Pupil Premium Toolkit was our response.

Our challenge is the tendency for the divide between the education haves and have-nots to widen in the classroom. It is termed the Matthew Effect after the biblical reference: 'For unto everyone that hath shall be given, and he shall have abundance; but from him that hath not shall be taken away even that which he hath' (Matthew, XXV).

The effect is observed in many aspects of teaching. It is seen among young children learning to read (Stanovich, 1986). Pupils who fall behind in reading read less, lagging further behind their peers. Poor reading skills then inhibit their learning in other subjects. They are consigned to be education's losers.

Disadvantaged students are more likely to be selected into lower sets – even when they have demonstrated strong academic potential. They suffer the double whammy of missing out on the most effective teachers and the knock to their sense of self-worth. The more rigid the setting, the more divisive it is.

We also highlight where approaches can push back against education's prevailing wind. Peer tutoring can boost the progress of low-achieving pupils and pupils from low-income backgrounds. Metacognitive approaches that make learning goals explicit often help lower-attaining pupils more than their classmates who are already successful.

Teachers need to be conscious of the myriad ways in which disadvantage manifests itself among children. We are not just talking about crude indicators of deprivation such as whether pupils qualify for free school meals, or whether they are designated as having special educational needs or disabilities. When you are born, as well as where and how you are born, has a profound impact on your education prospects. Children born between June and August have lower self-esteem, are less confident in their own abilities and are more prone to fall into risky behaviour. If we aspire to have an equitable school system, then we must address summer-born disadvantage.

The prize of great teaching is progress for pupils from less privileged backgrounds. The most effective teachers succeed with all of the pupils in their class, regardless of their background (Kyriakides et al., 2018). In classes with less effective teachers, disadvantaged pupils fall even further behind. The typical difference between more effective and less effective teachers is about three months more progress in the classes of successful teachers (Hanushek and Rivkin, 2010). We can always do better. How can we target more of the practices we know are good learning bets? Is there a particular pedagogy of poverty – types of teaching that benefit children from less supportive environments outside schools? This book offers some tentative answers to these challenges, which have bedevilled schools for decades. Targeted one-to-one or small-group tutoring, for example, can be used for catch-up (see page 29).

There are also effective programmes enabling children to be better prepared for learning – providing free breakfasts, offering sleep education and ensuring they get glasses for poor eyesight (see page 97). Perhaps schools could pledge to provide a basic package for children. This would have a particular education lens – teaching pupils how to sit around a table when eating, for example. At the same time, there needs to be a clear marker in the sand to say what schools can't do, particularly when budgets are getting ever more stretched. We worry about schools becoming distracted by having to prepare pupils for learning, leaving less time for the learning itself.

Threshold Effect

A threshold effect is a sudden and radical change in a phenomenon, which occurs after surpassing a limit, called the threshold. A positive version is critical mass – once you have enough of something there is a qualitative change. A negative version is 'the straw that broke the camel's back'. When a limit is reached something breaks or stops working.

For example, when a teacher surpasses a level of pedagogical content knowledge in maths, further increases are only incremental for classroom learning. But below that level, learning suffers (Hill et al., 2005). It's critical that teachers understand the subject well enough to recognise the frequent misconceptions that stymie children's progress. Meanwhile, smaller classes are associated with only very small learning gains until they are well under 20 pupils. This appears to be the natural threshold below which teachers can change the way they teach – gathering more individual feedback from pupils in smaller groups.

More is not always better in teaching. More digital technologies and tools, from mobile phones to interactive displays, have diminishing returns and can distract from core teaching. Short bursts of phonics with frequent repetition until pupils gain fluency is the best approach (Sobel et al., 2011). Avoid teaching what pupils already know. It's a waste of time.

Becoming a great teacher – two metaphors

We hope this book will offer some useful tips for teachers developing their practice. Learning to teach is complex. You are trying to organise 30 children while undertaking activities enabling them each to learn new skills, knowledge or understanding, taking into account the short-term and long-term effects of your actions. The teacher is responsible for teaching across a broad curriculum. The challenge is as much about coordination as success for a particular objective.

Two metaphors may be useful to consider. Both emphasise that human activity is as much art as it is science. Compare learning to teach with the much simpler task of learning to drive, for example – involving one person and one car. The first lesson is overwhelming, during which you are thinking about speed, gears, mirrors, steering and braking all at the same time as thinking about following directions. But little by little as you practise and become fluent in each of the separate skills, you can then focus on coordinating these skills to get where you want to go. After a while it becomes second nature and you hardly have to think about the process of driving in your daily commute. Good teaching can appear effortless but much work will have gone into it.

Another useful metaphor is learning to cook. As amateur cooks, we build up a repertoire of recipes and techniques we are confident with and where we know the ingredients we use to prepare particular dishes and meals. An expert chef has had more formal training in learning how to use specific cooking techniques, for example in preparing the classic French sauces, béchamel, espagnole, hollandaise, tomate and velouté. These are often called the 'mother' techniques because they have produced a huge range of variants based on each of the core recipes. Chefs know how to prepare these, but also what dishes they complement and which ingredients work well with each.

Teaching skills and techniques are like this. There are some classic pedagogical tools and techniques, such as explaining, demonstrating, modelling and questioning, which form the basic repertoire of all teachers' work. There are also other key organisational strategies in, say, collaborative learning. These range from 'think, pair, share' (see www.readingrockets.org/strategies/think-pair-share), to more involved techniques like jigsaw groups or Kagan's collaborative structures (see www.kaganonline.com/free_articles/research_and_rationale/330/The-Essential-5-A-Starting-Point-for-Kagan-Cooperative-Learning).

You can often use different ingredients or processes but there is a limit to how much you can play with the basic recipe. Some have more flexibility or 'tolerance' than others. The proportions and timings for pastry are more precise than for a casserole. Soufflés are notoriously difficult to master, even the basic recipe. Teaching is similar. Some teachers develop a high level of expertise in different techniques and different task content or subject matter. They get a great match between the pedagogy, the content and the learners and serve up a delicious and nourishing lesson.

But TV's *The Great British Bake Off* reminds us of the difficulty of this challenge. Each contestant has the same ingredients, recipe and equipment. It is a great test of culinary skill. When in teaching do we have the opportunities to learn a new pedagogical technique and to practise it with different content and different settings so we can become experts? It is your skill in combining and 'cooking' the components that leads to effective learning rather than a soggy lesson.

Final words

The overarching message in this book confirms what all good teachers know. What matters most is the classroom interaction between teacher and pupil: providing and receiving effective feedback that moves learning on; encouraging independent learning through metacognitive or thinking about thinking strategies; providing one-to-one (or indeed two-to-one or three-to-one) tuition for children falling behind their peers. Structural changes in schools – reducing class sizes or launching new types of schools – have little impact on children's progress. But there is a catch: the closer you get to classroom interaction, the more the Bananarama Principle applies – it's how you do it that counts.

The principle operates at a deeper level. Research indicates the beliefs of teachers – why they adopt particular practices, the purposes they aim to achieve and their theories about how learning occurs – matter for the progress of their pupils. In other words, 'it ain't what you do, it's the why that you do it'. Effective teachers for example believe that all pupils are capable of making progress (Coe et al., 2014).

This book will enable teachers to think for themselves, rather than submit to the latest teaching fads, shiny new programmes or political edicts. Whether we like it or not, schools operate in an education marketplace and school leaders should assess the claims of specific programmes that come knocking at their door.

We also lay to rest the enduring myths that cling to the education system like barnacles on the bottom of a boat. The widespread belief that pupils have preferred learning styles doesn't stand up to scientific scrutiny. Allowing learners to discover key ideas for themselves also has no foundation in evidence. Praising pupils too much, far from boosting confidence, can convey a message of low expectations.

Leaders need to create an environment of trust and challenge – a place that fosters an open-minded and sceptical approach towards evidence about what has worked and – just as important – what hasn't worked. There is an ethical as well as economic imperative to do so. A challenge to any school head is to ask them, 'What have you stopped doing?' We urge teachers to compare not only the impact but the cost of what they do: 'It's not what you spend, but how you spend it that counts.' Schools manage tight budgets. Small-group tutoring for example may be a better bet than one-to-one tuition. You need to get the best education bang for your buck.

We want evidence to enrich and empower practice, not just inform it. *What Works?* doesn't promise magic medicine that will create perfect teaching, but it will help you navigate an uncertain world and improve the likelihood your school children will achieve their potential. It's in your hands. It's up to you. Just remember 'It ain't what you do, it's the way that you do it.'

HOW TO USE THIS BOOK

What Works? is divided into 21 chapters, each focussing on a common approach to teaching and learning. The chapters follow a consistent structure to enable you to dip in and out of the book to find the information you need when you need it.

Chapter overview

Each chapter begins with a table outlining the key points to provide an overview and summary of the information the chapter contains. The table includes an estimation of the effect size (positive or negative) of the approach, measured in the typical number of months' progress a class might be expected to make if the approach is implemented, based on the research and evidence available. For more information about how the effect size is calculated, see the technical notes on page xxii.

What is it?

The table is followed by a brief description of the approach or educational issue.

Does it work?

In this section, a description of the evidence of effectiveness is given, with additional information about the nature of this evidence and any variation in impact where this is available. Estimates are usually based on the evidence underpinning the toolkit. Where other evidence is used this is made clear in the text. There is also a discussion of any additional learning benefits the approach may have, aside from attainment gain, for example better behaviour or improved social interaction.

How does it work?

We often don't know the precise mechanisms that make things work in the classroom, but here we will discuss how the approach *might* work effectively in practice. We will look at each of the key principles underpinning the successful implementation of the approach, for example Bananarama, Goldilocks or the Matthew Effect (see page xiv), to help you understand how you can put the approach into practice with the best chance of success.

Useful quotes

We've added some relevant quotations in boxes throughout the text to explain, highlight and entertain.

Unexpected finding

There is often a counterintuitive finding, or just something surprising, in the evidence, and we share this with you here. Well, they surprised us!

Teaching tips

In each chapter, we've provided a series of tips and suggestions to help teachers turn the evidence into successful classroom practice. Remember these aren't guaranteed to work for all pupils every time, but they are your best bets based on the research available.

Leadership tips

We know that leadership is important in embedding evidence in schools. Sometimes approaches can be hard to use without a whole-school approach and leadership support. In this section, we provide practical guidance to help middle and senior leadership teams use the evidence to transform practice across their department or school.

Key readings

We've suggested other readings, both academic and practical, to take your thinking forward. If you want to know more, explore these texts to keep finding out about the topic or issue.

WHAT WORKS? OR WHAT'S WORKED? SOME TECHNICAL NOTES

Overview

The evidence we have used for this book comes mainly from about 200 reviews of education research, each summarising 50 or more reports of individual studies. Most of these include hundreds of pupils. These studies are a particular kind of review called a 'meta-analysis'. This is where a researcher has gathered as many studies as possible on a topic and combined or 'pooled' the findings. They are used in many fields, particularly medical studies, although the technique was first developed in education (Higgins, 2018). This is the same research that is used in the *Sutton Trust-EEF Teaching and Learning Toolkit*, though at times we have supplemented this with other studies where we felt it was important to explain or go beyond what is included in this.

It is important to understand the nature of the research evidence to use it well. Where we have drawn in wider evidence, we have made this clear in the text and we have supplemented this with citations which will take you to specific studies. The toolkit considers experimental evidence as being stronger than other research designs in terms of cause and effect. Sometimes we don't have this kind of evidence, such as for effective teaching or summer-born children, and we rely on correlational studies where researchers have looked at patterns of effects and their association with pupils' progress. You couldn't randomly assign children to be born in a particular month, but you can look at the progress children make who are born at different times of the year.

Good bets

We use the approach described above, using reviews, because this is the best way to get an overview of the evidence. Single studies, no matter how well designed and run, will never be definitive in education. There is too much variation in context, between teachers, pupils, schools and subjects, for universal educational laws to be identified from research. But we believe there are useful patterns of effects when you look across studies. This is particularly true if we try to work out the *typical* result of a programme or approach. It gives us an indication of whether an approach is a 'good bet' or not. If something tends to be successful when we look at the overall picture, then this is worth knowing. It does not guarantee it will work for you, in your school with your pupils, but it is a guide to what you might expect. It is what's worked, not what will work. Research evidence can help you find this, by picking out the patterns of findings across many studies. The research tells us what's worked, on average.

On average

As Dylan Wiliam (2006) has said, 'everything works somewhere and nothing works everywhere'. The challenge is working out what will work for you. It does mean some of the things that tend to be unsuccessful may be made to work in your context. This is unlikely, at least on average, and you will have to buck the trend. But if you can see why it might be a good solution in your context, and you are prepared to take the risk, then it still might be successful. You will have to be above the average to make it work, but this is not impossible. Some teachers somewhere will have succeeded with it; you just need to be like them. From this viewpoint, approaches like the *Sutton Trust-EEF Teaching and Learning Toolkit* give you a risk register, showing what has been successful or unsuccessful in other contexts. The higher the level of impact, the lower the risk. You just have to do something as well as the average study to make it work for you. The lower the impact, the more exceptional you need to be to succeed. An approach may be a risky outsider, but if you have insider knowledge, you may be able to make it work for you and your pupils. You need to have a clear rationale for this, and you will have to be careful not to fall into any traps.

Months' progress

A meta-analysis combines the average effect from all of the studies it includes. Our estimates of impact come from the *Sutton Trust-EEF Teaching and Learning Toolkit*. The toolkit takes the average 'effect size' from the different meta-analyses and converts this to the typical months of progress a class might expect to make if an approach is successfully implemented (EEF, 2018i). The effect size for a single study comes from a translation of the original test scores onto a scale or ratio based on the typical spread of scores (the standard deviation). It uses the progress pupils typically make in a year for the conversion. This was based on data from national tests in England as well as other sources (Higgins, 2018). It is only a broad approximation and is based on a number of assumptions. The main one is that any underlying variation or bias is evenly distributed across the toolkit. We know that some features of research influence the estimate of effect:

- Larger studies tend to have smaller effect sizes.
- Studies with younger learners or those with special educational needs tend to have larger effects (the spread of scores is narrower in these studies).
- It is easier to show improvement in simpler outcomes (e.g. vocabulary or spellings) than more complex ones (such as reading comprehension or extended writing).

This can influence or 'bias' an area of research. The toolkit assumes there is enough evidence of different types in each area. It is not ideal, but better than the other options. Effect sizes are difficult to interpret. What does a gain of 0.2 standard deviation units mean? Months' progress gives a more intuitive overall feel for the impact on learners in school. But this is a translation of a translation.

Try translating something in Google from French to Russian to English and you'll see what we mean.

The table below sets out the conversion used in the EEF Toolkit. This conversion is based on assuming pupils make about one standard deviation of progress per year and dividing this up into months. It is an approximation as pupils do not neatly progress in a smooth linear fashion, day by day, week by week and month by month. Also progress changes over time: younger pupils tend to progress more quickly, while older learners' progress slows down.

An example of this is in reading. In the first few years children master the alphabetic code, the orthography of the English language and its lexicography for early reading. Meaning and comprehension quickly follow allowing learners not just to learn to read more effectively, but also to read to learn. Contrast this with a typical 12-year-old. Their vocabulary and comprehension will still develop, particularly across the curriculum but not at the same rate.

At the same time the spread of learners increases. Some learners race ahead; others progress much more slowly. Each year this gap widens. To get an effect size we 'standardise' the gain by the spread, so for older learners we are dividing by a larger number so tend to get a smaller effect size.

To some extent these issues balance out. Effect sizes reduce as learners get older, but then so does progress, so the months scale is not as unbalanced as it might seem. You can use the scale in either direction. If you know the effect size you can read off the months; if you know the months you can see the range of effects.

Months' progress	Effect size from...	... to	Description
0	-0.01	0.01	Very low or no effect
1	0.02	0.09	Low
2	0.10	0.18	Low
3	0.19	0.26	Moderate
4	0.27	0.35	Moderate
5	0.36	0.44	Moderate
6	0.45	0.52	High
7	0.53	0.61	High
8	0.62	0.69	High
9	0.70	0.78	Very high
10	0.79	0.87	Very high
11	0.88	0.95	Very high
12	0.96	>1.0	Very high

Summary

Evidence is about what's worked, not what will work for you. You have to decide what fits your context and your own skills and capabilities as a teacher. We use averages of averages, with all of the mathematical risks involved. There is always a spread of effects, so this gives us an indication of good bets and risky outsiders. It's the best we can do to make judgements about the relative effects of different approaches – at least at the moment.

IMPROVING CLASSROOM TEACHING

Attainment gain	+ 4 months	
Learning benefits	• Improved child outcomes including independent thinking, self-esteem, confidence, grit and problem-solving skills.	
Unexpected finding	• Praising pupils too much hinders learning.	
Teaching tips	• Measure teaching by the pupil progress made. • Create an environment of trust to challenge and develop practice. • Try reciprocal observations in pairs or triads. • Target support where understanding of student misconceptions is weak. • Provide clear, specific and challenging goals. • Use a mentor to mediate feedback.	
Leadership tips	• Frame observations as a formative process enabling teachers to improve practice. • Share your own challenges to promote a culture of trust and professional learning. • Use findings from observations and student data with caution. • Agree a school-wide definition of what makes great teaching. • Consider teaching guides published in specific subjects. • Use senior leaders and external advisors as observers sparingly.	
Principles	• Bananarama • The Matthew Effect • Threshold Effect	

WHAT IS IT?

We begin by going beyond the scope of the *Sutton Trust-EEF Teaching and Learning Toolkit*, which examines specific teaching practices, to draw out a general lesson about the importance of teaching from the wider research about effective teaching and learning. Improving teaching involves three challenges: defining what great teaching is; observing and measuring it; and providing feedback to improve it. Each stage is far from simple. It's hard to do. There is no basic recipe for effective classroom teaching. It has been described as the most complex human activity ever invented (Shulman, 2004). A review of over 200 studies concluded great teaching is simply that which leads to improved student progress (Coe et al., 2014).

Getting teachers to observe each other's classroom practice in an atmosphere of trust and challenge is a good start, but this isn't an exact science: even experienced teachers disagree on what good teaching looks like. The practice of observation benefits both observers and observed. Watching other teachers makes you reflect on your own teaching skills and methods. Triads of teachers each taking it in turns to teach and observe can be a powerful way of improving practice in a trusted but

> **'Classroom teaching… is perhaps the most complex, most challenging, and most demanding, subtle, nuanced, and frightening activity that our species has ever invented.'**
>
> Lee Shulman (2004)

challenging environment. The long-term benefits for professional development may not be seen immediately, but studies have found teachers working in schools with supportive professional environments continued to improve after three years – challenging the claim that all teachers improve at first but then plateau (Coe et al., 2014). Teachers in less supportive schools declined in their effectiveness.

Conclusions from multiple observations by well-prepared observers should be triangulated with other measures – data on student progress and surveys of pupil feedback. Assessing teaching should be a formative process, helping teachers to develop their skills and knowledge. Many teachers find it difficult giving precise and honest feedback to fellow teachers. The principles here are the same as giving feedback to students. It needs to be timely, focussed, positive, and should guide the way forward. This last step is frequently missed, and the learning opportunity lost.

DOES IT WORK?

Great teaching is that which leads to greater student progress. Having an effective teacher rather than an average teacher raises a pupil's attainment by a third of a GCSE grade across a range of subjects. In maths, one year with an effective teacher has been found to boost performance by 25–45 per cent – this would be the equivalent to a learning gain of about three to five months found in studies in the *Sutton Trust-EEF Teaching and Learning Toolkit*. These studies don't identify the characteristics that make up great teaching, but simply demonstrate that pupil progress varies for different teachers (Sutton Trust, 2011).

The potential effects may also be significant for pupils from disadvantaged backgrounds, with some studies even suggesting they can gain an extra year's worth of learning during a year with very effective teachers compared with less effective teachers (Sutton Trust, 2011).

However, improving teachers' effectiveness is not easy. Trials of teacher observation programmes in English schools have failed to match the immediate gains in student progress seen in other countries. One reason for this could be that normal teaching practice in comparison schools in England is already effective so the programmes add little extra immediate advantage (see box overleaf). We have little data quantifying the likely long-term benefits of such programmes.

 ## Learning benefits

Effective teaching can be measured by progress in many valued outcomes – not just test results. It might include improvements in independent thinking, self-esteem, confidence, grit or articulacy. Good teaching develops children in the whole; it is not teaching to the test (see more on this in the afterword, page 125). We might also look at the kinds of outcomes employers value, such as problem-solving, team work and being able to take responsibility. We often forget that, whether we like it or not, we are teaching these things both explicitly and implicitly in the ways we choose to teach in our schools.

HOW DOES IT WORK?

Assessing good (and great) teaching should cover at least six components (Coe et al., 2014): pedagogical content knowledge, quality of instruction, classroom climate, classroom management, teacher beliefs and professional behaviours. Each component is explored in more depth on pages 4 and 5. There is strong evidence that knowing a subject well and commanding core instructional skills lead to improved learning. We have weaker evidence of impact on student results for the other skills and attributes. This doesn't make them less important; it may be down to a lack of research.

There is no set way in which these six components combine to make up good practice. There isn't one kind of teaching effectiveness. Two teachers with different skills, knowledge and understanding may have similar impact on pupils. Different attributes could be important at different times. Master teachers are adept improvisers, knowing what to do when and for whom.

The six dimensions of pedagogy

Below is a starter kit for thinking about how effective your pedagogy is. The six dimensions were developed from a review of research and published guides of teaching effectiveness. You can use the list to reflect on your own practice. Which areas are you already doing well and which could be strengthened? Could you use the six dimensions to develop a school- or department-wide plan to improve teaching in every classroom?

1. Pedagogical content knowledge

It isn't enough to know in depth the material being taught. Teachers must get inside the minds of pupils and understand how they think about a subject. They need to see what it looks like from the pupils' perspective as they traverse cul-de-sacs, wrong turns and steep curves in their learning journey.

2. Quality of instruction

Great teachers are on-the-go orchestrators of learning, knowing when to prod and prompt, when to go fast and slow, and when to focus one-to-one or whole class. They command a repertoire of tools – questioning, assessing progress, reviewing previous learning, providing model responses, allowing adequate time for practice to embed skills, and progressively introducing new learning (scaffolding). Effective instruction is all about enabling pupils to take the next steps in their own learning.

3. Classroom climate

Great teachers perform a delicate balancing act. They create a climate of high expectations, but aren't so demanding they damage pupils' self-esteem. They link the success and progress of students to the efforts they make, rather than their apparent ability. They value resilience to failure, or grit.

4. Classroom management

Learning flourishes under the right conditions. Great teachers exude a calm authority – clamping down on misbehaviour and consistently enforcing the lines pupils can't cross. Failure to discipline an unruly minority means less learning for the majority. Planning lesson time and classroom space are also important.

5. Teacher beliefs

Effective teachers are believers in human potential. One study found better maths results from teachers who believed all pupils are able to become numerate (Askew et al., 1997). It's not just how you teach but why you teach that matters.

6. Professional behaviours

Teachers should take part in collaborative professional activities that enhance their practice. They should reflect on and evaluate what they do, consider evidence and research and invest in their own development with other colleagues. Time spent away from the classroom improves learning.

Ten teaching myths

Classroom myths and misconceptions lurk in schools like viruses – as one unfounded practice is exposed, another fad rears its ugly head. When it comes to improving teaching, we yearn for easy answers and quick wins. Myths are tempting as they sound scientific and often make intuitive sense, but behind many lie multi-million-pound industries, preying on vulnerable teachers.

Be on your guard at all times.

Here we list ten common classroom myths that endure despite widespread debunking by researchers. It's important to consider what you may be doing that doesn't work – as well as what might work. Stopping doing things that are ineffective or inefficient frees up more time for the classroom teaching that is likely to make a genuine difference.

1. Group learners into sets

Grouping children into sets according to their current performance makes little difference to learning outcomes – and this is the case in maths, where setting is common, as in other subjects (Gamoran, 1992). In theory, it allows teachers to target a narrower range of pace and content during lessons. But in practice it creates an exaggerated sense that pupils are at the same level. Teachers can go too fast with

> 'It is our choices, Harry, that show what we truly are, far more than our abilities.'
>
> Albus Dumbledore (Rowling, 1998)

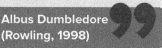

the high sets and too slow with the low sets. Schools also do not actually test for ability; they group on current performance. Otherwise you wouldn't have so many summer-born children in what are called 'low-ability' sets. Does being born in August make you less capable than being born in September? See more on academic setting on page 77.

2. Encourage re-reading and highlighting to memorise key ideas

Re-reading and highlighting are among the most common and apparently most obvious ways to memorise or revise. They give a deceptive feeling of being on top of the material. However, a range of studies have shown that testing yourself, trying to generate answers and creating intervals between study to allow forgetting are all more effective approaches (Dunlosky et al., 2013).

3. Improve confidence and aspirations before teaching content

Attempts to boost the motivation and confidence of pupils before teaching them new material won't achieve much (Gorard et al., 2012). The impact on subsequent learning is close to zero. Children become demotivated if they are failing in class. If they can succeed academically, they may gain confidence as well. There is a close relationship between aspiration and achievement. Boosting achievement gives the learner a realistic chance of raising aspiration. Think of this as a spiral interaction: increase achievement – raise aspiration – increase achievement – raise aspiration.

4. Teach learners in their preferred learning style

The widespread belief that students can be classified as visual, auditory or kinaesthetic learners is persistent, despite several reviews debunking learning styles (Geake, 2008; see page 73 for more on learning styles). One survey found over nine in ten teachers agreed with the claim that individuals learn better when they receive information in their preferred learning style (Howard-Jones, 2014). Yet the evidence is clear: there are no benefits from this approach (Riener and Willingham, 2010; Pashler et al., 2008). Vary the way you present information, and encourage learners to understand their strengths and capabilities, but do not limit learners by targeting what you think is their 'style'.

5. Ensure learners are active not passive

Beware 'learning pyramids'. They detail precise percentages of material that will be retained when different activities are employed, or formulae showing how much people remember of what they hear, read and see. These percentages are pure fiction. If you want students to remember something you have to get them to think about it. This can be achieved by being physically 'active' or 'passive'. You can't see students' brains moving! Brain Gym is the name of a programme based on the idea that moving leads to optimal learning for children – termed 'educational kinesiology'. The founders claim the programme can help improve memory, concentration and intelligence. But this is backed by zero evidence (Watson and Kelso, 2014). If your lesson is so dull that learners need regular breaks from it, then think about the activities and their timing and pacing.

6. Digital technology increases boys' motivation and engagement

Yes, but it also improves girls' motivation and engagement too. There is very little difference between the sexes in terms of the impact of digital technologies on motivation. The key question is: does it increase pupils' motivation to learn? Or is playing with technology just more fun than normal lessons? Technology can be used in a range of ways to support learning, but a more 'engaged' class may not actually be learning any faster or more efficiently. See page 83 for more on digital technologies.

7. Teaching assistants don't help pupils to progress

It's true that poorly managed and prepared teaching assistants have little impact on learning (Blatchford et al., 2009). But that's the whole point: they need to be managed by teachers, and be prepared and trained. TAs can be invaluable secondary educators. See more about teaching assistants on page 25.

8. Reducing class sizes improves learning

Reducing class sizes has surprisingly limited impact on pupils (see page 87). Smaller classes work when teachers change the way they teach, catering to individual needs of pupils and receiving more feedback from children. It's not reducing class size that matters, but how you adapt teaching style with fewer pupils. That's why little impact is observed until class size is reduced to under 20 or even below 15 pupils per teacher.

9. It's always good to praise pupils

Praising pupils can feel like the right thing to do — affirming the work of learners. But studies suggest the wrong kinds of praise can do more harm than good (Dweck, 1999). Praise meant to be encouraging and protective of low-attaining students conveys a message of low expectations. Criticism of poor performance can indicate a teacher's high expectations. Praise is valued more when it is meaningful and less frequent. It's also more productive to praise a pupil's work or effort than make judgements about them as a person (Hattie and Timperley, 2007). Pupils will value being praised if they think they deserve it. It is not so much about praise given (by the teacher) as praise received (by the learner). See page 13 for more on the challenge of effective feedback.

10. Allow learners to discover things for themselves

There is no evidence that discovery learning works better than other approaches (Kirschner et al., 2006). The theory is that pupils will remember something if they discover it for themselves, but how easy is it to 'discover' French vocabulary and grammar? It may be possible, but it wouldn't be a good use of pupils' time. Studies suggest teachers should actively teach new ideas, knowledge or methods — so-called 'direct instruction' (Stockard et al., 2018) or 'explicit instruction' (Hollingsworth and Ybarra, 2017). But be aware that the term 'direct instruction' can mean different things to different people. In research terms, it is an approach that has clear objectives and uses tests and assessments to track progress and a range of strategies (including collaborative learning) to achieve mastery of these

> 'Any time that you, as a learner, look up an answer or have somebody tell or show you something that you could, drawing on current cues and your past knowledge, generate instead, you rob yourself of a powerful learning opportunity.'
>
> Bjork and Bjork (2011)

7

objectives. Additional teaching is provided until the targets are met. Of course, for younger children, developing familiarity with materials and their properties is an important part of learning about the world, but this does not mean that they can't also benefit from directed and guided interaction from an adult. See the chapter on mastery learning on page 51.

Measuring teacher effectiveness – tread carefully!

Published frameworks of teaching effectiveness are available, although a weakness of these is that attributes are broadly defined. Popular frameworks include Charlotte Danielson's 'Framework for Teaching', Robert Pianta's 'Classroom Assessment Scoring System' and Rosenshine's 'Principles of Instruction'. These may be good conversation starters to reach a school-wide agreement over what makes good

> **'High-stakes inference should not be based on lesson observation alone, no matter how it is done.'**
>
> Rob Coe (2014)

and great teaching. If you decide to use a framework, treat the results of subsequent observations as a guide. Much depends on the unique interactions between a teacher and their pupils. Learning is invisible, so we use signals to indicate it is happening – for example students being busy and engaged. Some types of behaviour may lead to higher gains among pupils, but they can't guarantee them.

One review suggests low-stakes judgements from lesson observations may be used if at least two observers independently observe a total of at least six lessons, provided those observers have been trained for two to three days and have been assessed (Coe, 2014). This approach could, for example, indicate areas for improvement for a teacher. High-stakes judgements – promoting or firing – would need more substantial evidence gathered over a longer period of time.

England's observation trials

Trials of observation schemes in English schools have shown no immediate extra benefits on student progress compared with standard practice in other schools. But teachers did report benefits for their practice.

In one programme, GCSE maths and English teachers were trained in observation (Worth et al., 2017). In a series of 20-minute observations over two years they rated peers on how they managed behaviour and communicated with students. Meanwhile primary school teachers undertook Lesson Study, a programme developed in Japan in which small groups of teachers co-plan lessons (Murphy et al., 2017). Teachers take it in turn to deliver a new lesson while their peers observe the impact on a few pupils. The teachers then reflect and plan again.

Teachers reported they felt uncomfortable taking time out for observations. And even schools undertaking more observations didn't demonstrate better pupil results. Teachers, however, rated the training highly, particularly in the Lesson Study approach, and felt it was good for their development. It may be that the impact will be demonstrated in later years when teachers have consolidated what they have learnt. The studies point to the crucial role of a coordinator, usually someone in the school's senior leadership team, to organise and champion the observations.

Other researchers have proposed the clinical supervision model used in medicine. This comprises a flow of observations with pre- and post-observation meetings (conferences). In the pre-observation conference, aims of the observation are negotiated. In the post-observation conference, feedback should be factual, non-threatening, constructive and aimed at creating reflective and self-directed teacher learners. It should take place in a comfortable setting no longer than five days after the observation.

Making judgements about teachers requires a range of measures, including observations and data on student progress. You should triangulate results against each other. A single source of evidence may suggest the way forward; when it is confirmed by another independent source it starts to become a credible guide. There is little evidence headteachers can judge teaching reliably or that it can be measured by assessing teacher self-reports, classroom artefacts and teacher portfolios.

Don't be fooled into thinking reams of student data equate to robust evidence – progress data can be affected by previous teachers, measuring errors and the different make-up of successive student cohorts. Gold-standard classroom observations identifying teachers as 'above' or 'below' average agree with student progress data only 60 per cent of the time. This compares with the 50 per cent we would get by tossing a coin (Coe et al., 2014).

The evidence suggests using a formative approach, based on continuous assessment and feedback rather than results from high-stakes tests (Timperley et al., 2007). Working alongside peers in an environment of trust and challenge is most productive – where a teacher being observed has full control over what happens to information about their observation. Evaluations by external advisors should be treated with healthy scepticism.

Feedback – closing learning loops

The same principles for feedback for student learning (see page 17) apply for teacher learning, but as with feedback in the classroom it is hard to deliver well. This key step in the teacher learning and development process is often missing.

Timperley (2008) and colleagues advocate a 'knowledge-building cycle'. This is a feedback loop for teachers associated with improved student outcomes.

Teachers should provide clear, specific and challenging goals for fellow teachers; they should focus on the learning rather than on the person and should not make comparisons with others. A good area to focus on is teachers' knowledge of subject content and how students learn it. Teacher learning can have a big impact on student outcomes when conducted in this way (Meissel, et al., 2016).

The key here is that learning loops are closed, so the teacher develops their practice:

- Have clear, realistic learning goals been articulated?
- Do you know the steps required for them to be achieved?
- Have you done enough to ensure the goals are met and learning can move on?

Principles

Principle 1: Bananarama

The history of education is littered with apparent panaceas that promised to transform teaching – from large-group instruction to small-group teaching, one-to-one tutoring, structured tutoring programmes, child-centred learning and direct instruction to name but a few. But the evidence is clear – although all of these things can work, what matters most is how well a teacher carries out these various approaches, not the approaches themselves. It matters how well they are planned, delivered and reviewed. Indeed, great teachers are characterised by knowing what to do when for what children. It is these choices that make the difference.

Principle 2: The Matthew Effect

The effects of high-quality teaching are large for pupils from disadvantaged backgrounds, who can gain up to an extra year's worth of learning during an academic year with very effective teachers compared to less effective teachers. If the best teachers work with the most vulnerable pupils, this has the potential to narrow the attainment gap.

Principle 3: Threshold Effect

Once a teacher reaches an adequate level of pedagogical content knowledge in maths, further increases do not make much difference; below that level, however, learning suffers (Hill et al., 2005). The most effective teachers command deep mastery of the subjects they teach. Teachers without a basic command of subject knowledge can't answer students' questions or understand the common misconceptions that block their progress. It's as if the teacher has entered a new country without learning the new language and is now trying to tell the inhabitants what to do.

Unexpected finding

There is a strong urge to want to make students feel positive about their work, particularly if they are struggling with new material, but studies suggest excessive praise can be harmful to learning (Dweck, 1999).

A student praised for completing an easy task can see this as a sign the teacher has low expectations. This hinders rather than helps their self-confidence. Meanwhile a student criticised for not doing as well can interpret this as a sign of high expectations. Praise should be sparing so its impact is not devalued. It should focus on what the pupil has achieved rather than judging them as a person. Praise relates to challenge. If a teacher sets a high level of challenge and the pupils accept this, then praise will be more meaningful.

Teaching tips

✓ Always measure your teaching by the pupil progress made – it's the only meaningful yardstick we have.

✓ Create an environment of trust with colleagues that allows you to challenge each other's thinking and practice.

✓ Try reciprocal observations and feedback in pairs or triads.

✓ Use the six dimensions of pedagogy to reflect with colleagues on different aspects of your teaching.

✓ Provide clear, specific and challenging goals for fellow teachers and see the learning cycle through so they reach their next steps. Target support for colleagues at particular areas where their understanding of student misconceptions is weak. This is a promising strategy for professional development.

✓ Use a mentor to mediate feedback in a supportive environment.

✓ Beware the teaching myths!

Leadership tips

✓ Lead by example – share your own development needs and challenges to promote a culture of trust and professional learning across the school.

✓ Frame teacher evaluation as a formative process, enabling teachers to work together to improve their practice.

✓ Use findings from observations and student data with caution – primarily for helping teachers to improve.

✓ Look at the recognised frameworks and the six dimensions of teaching effectiveness to develop an agreed school-wide definition of what makes great teaching. This could be published as a poster for all to see.

✓ Try pairing general measures of teacher effectiveness with published frameworks for specific content in particular subjects. These can have more impact on student learning. Guides have been published for languages, art, maths and science at https://ies.ed.gov/ncee/wwc/practiceguides.

✓ Train teachers in lesson observation and check their progress.

✓ Use senior leaders and external advisors as observers sparingly and for specific tasks.

KEY READINGS

Academic

Murphy, R., Weinhardt, F., Wyness, G. and Rolfe, H. (2017), 'Lesson Study: Evaluation report and executive summary'. London: EEF. https://educationendowmentfoundation.org.uk/public/files/Projects/Evaluation_Reports/Lesson_Study.pdf

Timperley, H., Wilson, A., Barrar, H. and Fung, I. (2007), 'Teacher professional learning and development'. Wellington: Ministry of Education. www.oecd.org/education/school/48727127.pdf

Worth, J., Sizmur, J., Walker, M., Bradshaw, S. and Styles, B. (2017), 'Teacher observation: Evaluation report and executive summary'. London: EEF. https://educationendowmentfoundation.org.uk/public/files/Projects/Evaluation_Reports/Teacher_Observation.pdf

Practical

Coe, R. (2014), 'Classroom observation: It's harder than you think', *CEM Blog*, www.cem.org/blog/414/

Coe, R., Aloisi, C., Higgins, S. and Major, L. E. (2014), 'What makes great teaching? Review of the underpinning research'. London: Sutton Trust. https://suttontrust.com/wp-content/uploads/2014/10/What-Makes-Great-Teaching-REPORT.pdf

Cordingley, P., Higgins, S., Greany, T., Buckler, N., Coles-Jordan, D., Crisp, B., Saunders, L. and Coe, R. (2015), 'Developing great teaching: Lessons from the international reviews into effective professional development'. London: Teacher Development Trust.

Ofsted (2018), 'Six models of lesson observation: An international perspective', https://assets.publishing.service.gov.uk/government/uploads/system/uploads/attachment_data/file/708815/Six_models_of_lesson_observation.pdf

② EFFECTIVE FEEDBACK FOR LEARNING

 Attainment gain

+ 8 months

 Learning benefits

- Boosts the confidence of pupils and their belief they can succeed; pupils must overcome perceived threats to take leaps in learning.
- Builds a climate of trust in the classroom through which greater challenge can be provided.

 Unexpected finding

- Feedback can make things worse!

 Teaching tips

- Tell learners when they are right (and why) more than when they are wrong.
- Show learners where they have improved.
- Praise selectively.
- Use digital feedback where appropriate.
- Provide feedback for challenging tasks.
- Develop peer feedback.

 Leadership tips

- Focus on feedback received, not feedback given.
- Frame observations as opportunities for peer observation and professional learning.
- Develop whole-school agreement on the extent of feedback and markers of quality.
- Develop peer feedback strategies across the school.

 Principles

- Bananarama
- Goldilocks

WHAT IS IT?

Feedback is information given to the learner and/or the teacher about the learner's performance relative to the learning goals, which can then redirect the teacher's and the learner's actions to achieve the goal. It is the crucial second step in teaching after initial instruction. It can be verbal, written or given through tests – and it's challenging to get right. The key issue is not the feedback given by the teacher; it is the feedback received (and acted upon) by the learner.

This can come from a variety of sources, not just the teacher – from other adults, like teaching assistants (page 25), from older pupils (see peer tutoring, page 45), from digital technology (page 83), or from each other (see collaborative learning, page 109). The aim is to get learners to internalise this feedback so that they can monitor and improve their own learning (see metacognition and self-regulation, page 35).

> **'No one can be sure that the message they contain will one day find a receiver.'**
>
> Eleanore Hargreaves, likening teacher comments to bottles thrown into the sea (2011)

It's important to note that feedback is not just marking. Verbal feedback is usually more effective. Marking is only feedback when it changes what learners do next!

DOES IT WORK?

Providing specific, timely and focussed feedback can boost the learning of pupils by an extra eight months during an academic year. Recent trials in busy classrooms suggest more realistic gains of three to four months are achievable (EEF, 2017b). However, feedback interventions can also slow down learners. Feedback can be good but it can also be bad. It's how comments are delivered, received and acted upon that matters.

> **'The single biggest problem in communication is the illusion that it has taken place.'**
>
> George Bernard Shaw

The ultimate aim is to prompt deeper-level learning. Often the answer to 'where to next?' for students is 'more of the same' rather than deeper learning. Reflect on the questions you pose to pupils. Are you encouraging superficial learning rather than deeper understanding? Are your pupils committed to their learning goals?

Formative tests can be powerful vehicles for feedback, but you should aim for 'on-the-go' assessment, which shapes minute-by-minute and day-by-day classroom activity. In the Assessment for Learning (AfL) programme, techniques like traffic lights and WALT (we are learning today) and WILF (what I'm looking for) were overused. They became a shallow, tick-box assessment used to track how far students had advanced up a prescribed ladder of National Curriculum levels. This was far from the formative, on-the-go assessment it was intended to be, shaping classroom activity minute by minute and day by day. In practice, they lost their power to change the focus of interaction.

> **'In most of the classrooms we have studied, each student already knows about 40–50% of what the teacher is teaching.'**
>
> Graham Nuthall (2007)

Learning benefits

Feedback is an emotional and cognitive process. Students may face threats to their wellbeing when considering leaps in learning: the fear of losing face in front of their peers or the fear of getting a question wrong. Pupils will take one of two roads: the growth pathway to make learning gains or the wellbeing pathway to avoid threats. Learning gaps must therefore be large enough to extend learners but not so big that they are set up to fail. Pupils will make more effort if they believe ability is malleable rather than fixed, and if they are oriented towards mastery, or self-improvement, rather than performance, or how well they do compared with their peers. Find out more about how to do this effectively in the chapter on mastery learning (page 51).

Feedback shouldn't threaten pupils' beliefs in their ability to learn. Feedback from peers (Gielen et al., 2010) and from digital technology (Van der Kleij et al., 2015) is often seen as a lower threat than from a teacher or other adult with authority. It can also be easier to increase the quantity of feedback from peers and technology than from an already over-worked teacher.

HOW DOES IT WORK?

Effective feedback makes learning more efficient by changing what teachers and learners do next. It speeds up the learning process by identifying what the learner needs to do differently to succeed. It is about efficiency in the learning process, making sure the learners attend to what will help them most.

Feedback must feed forward. It works best when it contains clear next steps for the learner. It's important to be clear about what we mean by effective feedback. It can be represented in the following 'learning loop'. Learning occurs when learning loops are closed.

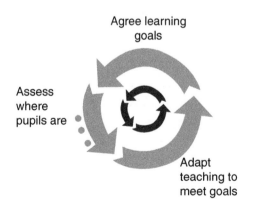

Figure 1 The learning loop

It's hard to do. Often goals are vague, assessment crude, and teachers don't adapt what they do. Goals are changed, abandoned or rejected altogether. It's so easy to slip into automatic or generic observations that don't address specific misunderstandings or knowledge gaps. Learners lose faith.

> 'I think it's very important to have a feedback loop, where you're constantly thinking about what you've done and how you could be doing it better.'
>
> **Elon Musk (2012)**

 # Principles

Principle 1: Bananarama

Pupils progress faster when they are told how they have got it right rather than how they have got it wrong. Teachers need to look for the impact of feedback on pupils' behaviour. How has it been received and understood? Focus on quality not quantity of marking. Remember that feedback can come from peers as well as adults.

Praising, rewarding or punishing pupils meanwhile has little effect. These comments or actions contain little information on how to move the learner forward to his or her goal. Goals should be specific and challenging, but tasks simple.

> 'In helping players improve their free-throw percentage, basketball coaches do not just tell the athletes to make sure that they get the ball through the hoop; they focus on mechanics such as reminding the athlete to bend their knees, and to keep the elbows tucked in.'
>
> **Dylan Wiliam (2011)**

The aim should be to progress from basic task or personal feedback to higher levels of feedback relating to learning strategies and how pupils self-regulate their own learning (see the chapter on metacognition and self-regulation, page 35). Avoid personal feedback – such as 'what a clever girl' – as it provides no information for moving learning on. Praise should be directed to increasing pupils' efforts to understand a problem: 'You're really great because you have completed this task by applying this concept.' For more complex tasks feedback can be delayed, but for simple tasks it should be immediate.

Three central questions that feedback must answer (Hattie and Timperley, 2007)

1. **Where am I going?**
   What are the learning goals? This could be 'passing a test' or 'completing an assignment', or it could be comparative, such as 'doing better than last time'.

2. **How am I going?**
   What progress is being made toward a learning goal?

3. **Where to next?**
   What needs to be done to make progress?

Principle 2: Goldilocks

Teachers should try to find a balance of challenging but sparing feedback. This means addressing faulty interpretations, rather than a total lack of understanding (which warrants more direct instruction instead). The details of how feedback drives learning are complex and the evidence is contradictory. You need to judge the nudge your feedback gives, as you can make things worse as well as better.

Some key points and examples of best practice when using feedback are summarised in the table below. It's split into four specific aspects you might be feeding back about: the task, the process, self-regulation and the individual.

Feedback about	Examples	Key points
The task	Feedback about how well the task is being achieved or performed, such as: • indicating where correct responses are different from incorrect • getting more or different information relevant to the task • building more task knowledge • prompts and direct cues.	• Feedback should focus even more on correct than incorrect behaviours, and should encourage the learner. • Be positive about errors as learning opportunities.
The process	Feedback specific to the processes of learning, the how rather than the what, or relating and extending tasks, such as: • identifying connections between ideas • developing strategies for spotting mistakes • explicitly learning from mistakes • offering cues to the learner about different strategies and errors.	• Identify where in the process to focus attention to improve relative to previous attempts.
Self-regulation	How students monitor, manage and regulate their actions towards the learning goal, such as: • their capability to identify feedback themselves and to self-assess • their willingness to put effort into seeking and dealing with feedback • having confidence they are correct • their positive attributions about success AND failure • how good they are at help-seeking.	• Emphasise success at challenging activities through effort, focussing on specific strategies for self-regulation which led to their success. • Self-corrected errors are a key part of this.

Feedback about	Examples	Key points
The individual	Praise directed to the effort, self-regulation, engagement or processes relating to the task or performance, such as: • 'You're really great because you have worked hard to complete this task by applying this concept', NOT 'good girl'.	• This is the most common but most dangerous kind of feedback. • It tends to be general and personal. • Feedback should emphasise what the individual has done (or could do), not who they are.

MARKING AND WRITTEN FEEDBACK

Marking can be summative or formative. It is not necessarily feedback. When the marks or comments change what learners do, it is feedback. If they don't or learners can't use it, it isn't feedback even if this is what you intended. Marking as feedback can be simple ticks and crosses indicating correct and incorrect work, along with other non-verbal forms drawing attention to something needing correction (such as underlining, circling or using smiley faces).

Marking as feedback can also be in written words giving praise ('Excellent') or rewarding effort ('Good try!'), or may be more complex information indicating what could be improved and how (formative feedback). The idea is to provide individualised feedback to learners efficiently and effectively.

> '**Marking has evolved into an unhelpful burden for teachers, when the time it takes is not repaid in positive impact on pupils' progress. This is frequently because it is serving a different purpose, such as demonstrating teacher performance or to satisfy the requirements of other, mainly adult, audiences.'**
>
> Independent Teacher Workload Review Group (2016)

Marking provides grading where a score (9 out of 10) or a grade (B+) is given.

When marking is used formatively, it can support learning (Black and Wiliam, 2010). The evidence for the impact of summative tests is less conclusive (Black et al., 2011). Precise estimates are hard to make for the impact of marking, as there are few rigorous studies in this area – other than including marking as a topic in the *Sutton Trust-EEF Teaching and Learning Toolkit*, the EEF published a review that showed the need for future research (EEF, 2016). We estimate that marking can add two months to pupils' learning in one year. This effect is derived from studies that have looked at summative feedback (Harlen and Deakin Crick, 2002) to provide an idea of how marking on its own might compare with the effects of other toolkit strands.

It is not the marking that has an impact on learners but the feedback it provides. It only works when pupils (or teachers) do something different as a result. A score might motivate a learner to work harder, but it might also make them slack off or become demotivated.

Marking may also help teachers assess and diagnose pupils' work, but so does just reading it or undertaking a systematic analysis of errors.

As we have already seen, feedback is difficult. It is part of the complex communication in classrooms involving the teacher and usually at least 20 pupils (Smith and Higgins, 2006). You have to judge the nudge you are giving to the learner to make sure it has the desired effect. If a learner is not motivated, it may be wasted effort. If the comments are too complicated, the learner won't know what to do. If it convinces them they can't succeed, it may undermine any positive message you were trying to give (Murtagh, 2014; see more in the chapter on mastery learning, page 51). Studies of learners' understanding and interpretation of marking suggest most of it is for teachers, schools and parents rather than being an efficient way to give feedback to learners.

Executed well, marking can encourage and challenge learners, boosting their belief that they can succeed. It needs to signal next steps in learning, highlight progress made and reward effort – otherwise it can undermine confidence.

Three golden rules for marking

The evidence suggests that what improves outcomes is descriptive comments about what is successful or correct and information about what learners haven't done correctly. Praise isn't always necessary, nor is it right to focus only on what is incorrect (see more in the section on praise in Chapter 1 on improving teaching, page 7). The learner also needs to be motivated to improve; if they are not then any marking or feedback may be like water running off a duck's back. It won't stick. When successful, marking provides enough information for the learner to work out what to do themselves (see the chapter on metacognition and self-regulation, page 35).

Follow these three golden rules to make sure your marking is just right:

1. **Keep it simple.** Provide enough guidance so the learner knows what to do next.
2. **Keep it direct.** Be clear about what you want the learner to do. This might be explicit and written down or it might be implicit, particularly if it's non-verbal.
3. **Keep them interested.** Do your learners care? There is no point spending hours on providing extensive written feedback if pupils aren't motivated to use the information.

Less is more

Remember, less is more and it is important to keep learners engaged. The more motivated they are, the easier it is to give feedback comments or marks the students will use to improve their work.

> **'You never know what is enough unless you know what is more than enough.'**
>
> **William Blake (1793)**

Marking that is not feedback rarely works and less is certainly more. Most students see marking as a summative judgement that they can't change. They see the mark or the grade and don't read anything else, or if they do they don't act on it. It is feedback given, but not received.

Black and Wiliam (1998) argue that formative comments are more effective than either marks alone or comments and marks (scores), as the mark trumps the comment. Other evidence suggests it is challenging to make any kind of formative feedback work well (Smith and Gorard, 2005). Developing marking and feedback that improves learning outcomes isn't straightforward (Kingston and Nash, 2011).

The workload test

Endless marking – alongside data inputting and lesson planning – has increased the workload burden of teachers. To cut your workload, try this three-question test:

1. Does the activity directly contribute to the quality of teaching and learning interactions – is it needed?

2. Do you have evidence that what you are undertaking impacts on pupil progress – is it impactful?

3. Could there be equally impactful approaches that take less time – is it time efficient?

Time-consuming approaches to marking such as triple marking fail the workload test. Equally, when producing lesson plans, ask: who are they for and do they justify the time spent? Too often plans are designed for 'box-ticking' paper trails rather than enlivening classroom activity. It's tempting to seek the perfect plan when what matters most is how you adapt your teaching practice on the go. Try collaborating with colleagues to develop joint schemes of work.

Meanwhile, data-strewn Excel spreadsheets can assume an authentic aura of authority, but offer only an indicative, partial picture of the lives of pupils. Is your school data rich but evidence poor? Remember you can only measure some things. Agree a school-wide policy on the use and limitations of data. Does assessment tracking improve outcomes, or are you simply watching inevitable progress: watching the grass grow or feeding, weeding and watering?

For your own wellbeing and the good of pupils you shouldn't spend more than ten hours a week on the three workload sins – marking, data inputting and lesson planning.

Marking of students' work should focus on quality not quantity – given the paucity of research showing which marking approaches work best (EEF, 2016). There is little justification for time-consuming approaches such as triple marking where teachers check pupils' responses to initial marks. Teachers need to consider how their marking contributes to timely, focussed feedback, which is then acted upon by pupils. Less can be more: comment on fundamental misunderstandings rather than careless mistakes; comments accepted and used by pupils are more powerful than grades. Other forms of marking are worth exploring, for example peer marking, group marking, using marking rubrics and self-assessment. They all take time to set up and maintain, but overall are much less time consuming than wading through piles of marking every weekend. They all also involve the learner in responding to the feedback.

Unexpected finding

Feedback can make things worse. Although the average impact on learning is high, there are several studies showing negative effects. Feedback may be a good bet for improvement, but it can have the opposite effect to what you intended. If feedback is mistimed, it can distract the learner from what they need to focus on. If feedback is not specific enough, the learner may misunderstand what to do. If it is too specific, they don't have to think about what to do. If they tried hard and interpret the feedback to mean they failed, it can demoralise.

If you think of feedback as a prompt for what you want the learner to think about and focus on next, you have to judge the nudge carefully and try not to fall into any of the above traps. This is why it is important to think about the feedback received rather than the feedback given.

Teaching tips

✓ Tell learners when they are right (and why) rather than when they are wrong. This is important for complex outcomes (such as writing) rather than simple ones (spelling or maths facts).

✓ Show learners where they have improved. This is better than telling them they are right.

✓ Praise when learning is challenging and in a way the learner values. This is better than discouraging or being too effusive.

✓ Use digital feedback where appropriate. It is often effective and learners don't see it as criticism.

✓ Provide feedback for challenging tasks but get the balance right. If the task is too hard, they won't understand the feedback. If it is too easy, they won't value a positive message.

✓ Develop peer feedback with techniques such as two stars and a wish. This should lead to self-assessment.

✓ Mark less: you don't have to do it all. Responding in depth to 30 pupils with extensive comments may make you feel better, but it is not a good use of your time. Use any time saved to think about what to do next with pupils to deepen their learning.

✓ Keep marking meaningful and productive. Many strategies work for a limited time. Traffic lights, marking codes and symbols, coloured pens, stickers and smiley faces all have a limited shelf life. Used judiciously they can keep written feedback productive. Overused and they decay like radioactive elements into lead.

✓ Develop other feedback strategies. Use different strategies and techniques to provide feedback, such as peer marking, group marking (with group targets) and using rubrics and self-assessment.

Leadership tips

✓ Encourage teachers to focus on how the pupils receive and interpret feedback, not how much feedback is given. Use opportunities for peer observation, professional learning and modelling of effective feedback between teachers to help embed this.

✓ Develop a whole-school agreement on what is expected for feedback with consistent markers of quality. These should change over the course of each term and should be different for different age groups.

✓ Develop peer feedback strategies across the school, which lead to better self-assessment and self-regulation.

✓ Ensure the time teachers spend marking pays off. Reading and evaluating pupils' work is essential. Marking is not. If you feel you need to have a record of what your teachers do then make sure it drives better learning. Don't kid yourself the pupils will use it. Most of them won't. Trust your teachers to make professional decisions based on informal evaluation and to decide how and when to provide written feedback to their pupils. If teachers can't or don't do this, it's time for some CPD.

✓ Balance consistency and progression for pupils. It is your job to protect your staff from excessive time spent marking. This takes courage. A whole-school marking policy may make you feel better, but unless this is developmental and increases the challenge pupils are set over the course of a school year for each age group, then it will become routine and ineffective.

KEY READINGS

Academic

Black, P. and Wiliam, D. (1998), 'Assessment and classroom learning', *Assessment in Education: Principles, Policy and Practice*, 5, (1), 7–74.

EEF (2016), 'A marked improvement', https://educationendowmentfoundation.org.uk/evidence-summaries/on-marking

Hattie, J. and Timperley, H. (2007), 'The power of feedback', *Review of Educational Research*, 77, (1), 81–112.

Kluger, A. N. and DeNisi, A. (1996), 'The effects of feedback interventions on performance: A historical review, a meta-analysis, and a preliminary feedback intervention theory', *Psychological Bulletin*, 119, (2), 254–284.

Smith, H. and Higgins, S. (2006), 'Opening classroom interaction: The importance of feedback', *Cambridge Journal of Education*, 36, (4), 485–502.

Practical

Australian Institute for Teaching and School Leadership, 'Spotlight: Reframing feedback to improve teaching and learning', www.aitsl.edu.au/docs/default-source/research-evidence/spotlight/spotlight-feedback.pdf?sfvrsn=cb2eec3c_12

Findlater, S. (2016), *Bloomsbury CPD Library: Marking and Feedback*. London: Bloomsbury Education.

Hattie, J. and Clarke, S. (2018), *Visible Learning: Feedback*. Abingdon: Routledge.

Higgins, S. (2011), 'Formative assessment and feedback to learners', *Better: Evidence-Based Education*, Spring, 8–9. Baltimore, MA: Centre for Research and Reform, Johns Hopkins University.

McGill, R. M. (2016), *Mark. Plan. Teach.: Save time. Reduce workload. Impact learning*. London: Bloomsbury Education.

Zierer, K. and Wisniewski, B. (2018), *Using Student Feedback for Successful Teaching*. Abingdon: Routledge.

3 TEACHING ASSISTANTS

 Attainment gain + 1 month

 Learning benefits
- Improved social and emotional outcomes.
- Better classroom behaviour.
- Lower teacher stress.

 Unexpected finding
- Ineffective deployment of TAs can lead to poorer progress for pupils with special educational needs.

 Teaching tips
- Plan for focussed support with clear objectives.
- Ensure effective monitoring of learning outcomes.
- Review who your TA supports on a regular basis.

 Leadership tips
- Plan the timetable to maximise one-to-one and small-group support by TAs.
- Ensure TAs are trained and supported for their role.
- Ensure there is time for liaison between the TA and the class teacher and/or SENCO.

 Principles
- The Matthew Effect
- Bananarama

WHAT IS IT?

Teaching assistants (also known as TAs or classroom support assistants) are adults who support teachers in the classroom. Their duties can vary from school to school, from providing administrative and classroom support to providing targeted academic help to individual pupils or small groups. In most classrooms they are an integral part of school life. How they are deployed makes a huge difference to the impact on pupils' learning (Blatchford et al., 2007).

DOES IT WORK?

TAs can make a difference to pupils' learning in school but the impact they have varies. When they provide general support and sit with low-attaining pupils in class, they are less likely to support learning (Rubie-Davies et al., 2010). They may be helping with behavioural issues and social interaction, but the evidence suggests this can mean the teacher takes their eye off that group's progress. By contrast, when TAs are trained and supported to provide intensive support either one-to-one or in small groups, they can make a difference to pupils' learning of up to four months over the course of a year (Sibieta et al., 2016).

 Learning benefits

> 'At secondary level the more contact pupils had with support staff the less individual attention they had from teachers.'
>
> Blatchford et al. (2009)

There are other benefits to having another adult in the classroom. Studies report lower levels of stress for the teacher, better classroom behaviour and improved social interaction in classrooms with teaching assistants (Rubie-Davies et al., 2010). These are important benefits that may have an impact on pupils' learning. It may also be that for some pupils the support a TA provides is essential for their inclusion. How are you focussing on a pupil's learning, and not just on their social and behavioural outcomes?

HOW DOES IT WORK?

Progress is all about effective time spent learning. How do you plan for TA time in whole-class teaching? Can you ensure targeted support according to need? Regular and frequent blocks of time are best for catch-up or keep-up programmes.

 Principles

Principle 1: The Matthew Effect

Targeted support can help to close the attainment gap and reverse the Matthew Effect. Identifying which pupils are struggling, and planning a programme of intensive support that has clear outcomes and is monitored, can make a real difference. This is best planned in intensive bursts over a term (e.g. three or four times a week for at least half an hour at a time for five or six weeks). If you use your TA to avoid working with your low attainers, you are letting them down. You have the expertise to support them so use it. If you just work with your successful pupils, the chances are you will make the attainment gap larger.

> 'Prompts from TAs frequently supplied pupils with the answer. This meant that the TAs were in a sense doing the work for the pupils and pupils did not therefore need to engage in thinking.'
>
> Rubie-Davies et al. (2010)

Principle 2: Bananarama

It is not having a TA that makes the difference but how you work with your TA to support your pupils' learning. This means ensuring you have planning and review time as part of your TA's paid hours. This is not always easy in a hectic school week but it's essential. How is your TA deployed at the beginning and end of lessons? Are they sitting watching or working with an individual or small group? Do you vary the groups they support?

Unexpected finding

The most shocking finding in the UK's Deployment and Impact of Support Staff (DISS) Project in 2009 was that pupils with special educational needs did less well in classes with a TA than those without a TA (even when controlling for other factors). It seems the teachers didn't track progress well enough because they spent less time with their most vulnerable pupils (Webster et al., 2010).

Teaching tips

✓ Plan for focussed support with clear objectives and over a limited time period. Identify a small number of pupils who will benefit from additional help, perhaps in writing or mathematics. Work with the TA to identify a clear set of targets with materials to support this over a few weeks.

✓ Ensure effective monitoring of learning outcomes for all pupils and change the plan if it isn't working. This is not just tracking progress; it is identifying areas of difficulty in specific areas of the curriculum and having a defined programme to address this. This diagnosis then forms the baseline to track progress. Review and change the pace after a couple of weeks. Can the programme be speeded up or does it need more consolidation? If this is the case increase the frequency of sessions rather than the length of each one (i.e. five times a week rather than three).

✓ Review who your TA supports on a regular basis: you are the expert so make sure you teach your most vulnerable learners. Who in your class needs the most support? You should keep some intensive support activities for yourself. The opportunity to assess and diagnose difficulty is essential in setting realistic but challenging targets. Can your TA work with a group for consolidation, whilst you focus on some in-depth teaching? This needs to be balanced with class needs, but for your most vulnerable learners it will provide an invaluable opportunity.

Leadership tips

✓ Plan the timetable to maximise one-to-one and small-group support by TAs. Which parts of the lesson can some children afford to miss? If your TA watches the whole-class introduction and whole-class plenary you've wasted 30 minutes they could have been working one to one.

✓ Ensure TAs are trained and supported for their role. Don't assume they know what to do, even if they are experienced. Learning how to manage a targeted intervention programme can be a valuable professional development opportunity for your TAs. It will offer them a chance to take responsibility for a specific area of the curriculum and to develop some expertise.

✓ Monitor pupils' progress; if support isn't effective, reorganise it. This means having a bank of quick and reliable assessment tools.

KEY READINGS

Academic

Webster, R., Russell, A. and Blatchford, P. (2015), *Maximising the Impact of Teaching Assistants*. Abingdon: Routledge.

Practical

Davie, E. (2017), *How to be an Outstanding Primary Teaching Assistant*. London: Bloomsbury Education.

EEF (2016), 'Making Best Use of Teaching Assistants Campaign', https://educationendowmentfoundation.org.uk/scaling-up-evidence/campaigns/making-best-use-of-teaching-assistants/

Maximising the Practice of Teaching Assistants (2009), 'The Deployment and Impact of Support Staff (DISS) Project', http://maximisingtas.co.uk/research/the-diss-project.php

④ ONE-TO-ONE TUITION

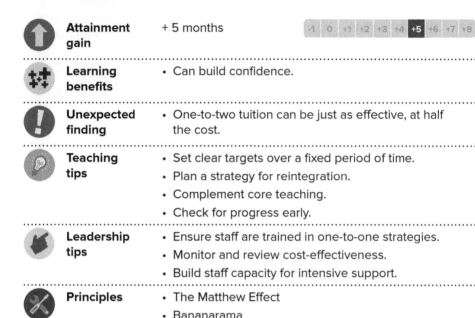

Attainment gain	+ 5 months		-1 0 +1 +2 +3 +4 **+5** +6 +7 +8
Learning benefits	• Can build confidence.		
Unexpected finding	• One-to-two tuition can be just as effective, at half the cost.		
Teaching tips	• Set clear targets over a fixed period of time. • Plan a strategy for reintegration. • Complement core teaching. • Check for progress early.		
Leadership tips	• Ensure staff are trained in one-to-one strategies. • Monitor and review cost-effectiveness. • Build staff capacity for intensive support.		
Principles	• The Matthew Effect • Bananarama		

WHAT IS IT?

One-to-one tuition involves a teacher, teaching assistant or other adult giving a single pupil intensive individual support. It may happen outside of normal lessons as extra teaching or as a replacement for other lessons. It involves direct teaching and feedback (see page 13). It differs from individualised learning (see page 103) where the learner is more independent and the emphasis is on tasks and activities the learner can undertake themselves, with the teacher in a monitoring role.

DOES IT WORK?

One-to-one tuition is a reliable way to help learners catch up if they are falling behind. Delivered well, it can lead to an extra five months learning gain for pupils during one academic year. The ability to target need and the intensity of support makes it very efficient (D'Agostino and Harmey, 2016). Benjamin Bloom (1984) used it as the benchmark for the greatest rate of progress a learner can make.

This research paper sets out the beginnings of approaches like John Hattie's (2008) *Visible Learning* and the *Sutton Trust-EEF Teaching and Learning Toolkit*, where the impact of different educational interventions are compared using effect sizes, or converted to other measures like months' progress. We have come a long way since 1984, but one-to-one remains an effective approach.

Primary schools are more effective at intensive support than secondary schools (Ofsted, 2009). This may be to do with greater flexibility in the timetable, or it may be to do with teachers' skills and knowledge about catch-up approaches.

> **'It was typically found that the average student under tutoring was about two standard deviations [twice the rate of progress] above the average of the control class (the average tutored student was above 98% of the students in the control class).'**
>
> Benjamin S. Bloom (1984)

Programmes involving trained teachers have twice the effect of those deploying teaching assistants or volunteers. One study found children who received tutoring from university undergraduates for primary school maths made three months' extra progress (EEF, 2018b). Professional development, training and structured guidance for practitioners are beneficial, and even more important for those less qualified and experienced.

One-to-one tuition is effective and can boost a pupil's capability and confidence (EEF, 2018c). However, it's important to remember their confidence may already have been affected by being picked out for extra support. Younger children may not notice this, but older pupils will be aware of the reasons for selection and this affects how they see themselves as learners. You need to be sensitive about how this is handled, particularly for older learners.

> **'I loved getting tutored and having that one-on-one attention that you sometimes do not get in regular school.'**
>
> Tia Mowry (2007)

Bear in mind that one-to-one tuition doesn't always work. Accurate diagnosis of need is important, as is the relationship between the tutor and tutee. It's also essential to monitor progress early to check it is working.

Learning benefits

One-to-one can provide targeted, intensive support that meets individual need. This can help build confidence and capability, which may be essential for overall progress.

HOW DOES IT WORK?

Benjamin Bloom argued it is the efficiency of one-to-one tuition that makes it so effective. The materials can be tailored to an optimal level of challenge for the learner and supported by the experienced tutor. There is very little remedial or corrective work needed on the part of the pupil. Bloom argued it was the level of appropriate instruction and feedback that made it so efficient. The learner works more intensively in a 20-minute one-to-one session than they do in whole-class or group work. They get through more material. They read or write more or do more maths. We should not underestimate the importance of successful practice and the development of fluency.

Principles

Principle 1: The Matthew Effect

Because one-to-one tuition is targeted, it is one of the few strategies that can close the attainment gap. Progress has to be more rapid, of course, than in class, but because the support can be targeted there is a chance for selected learners to be given extra support to catch up with their peers.

Principle 2: Bananarama

One-to-one tuition for catch up is a balancing act. On the one hand you want to help; on the other you are effectively saying you think your pupils are failing. The way that you do this is important. One-to-one is not a guaranteed solution – it doesn't always work. Sometimes the pupil is not receptive, or the person teaching is not attuned to the specific issues. Overall it is a good bet, but still needs some thought and careful planning.

> **'Let us remember: One book, one pen, one child, and one teacher can change the world.'**
>
> Malala Yousafzai

Although intensive one-to-one tuition is effective, there are other options to consider that provide intensive support to individual pupils (Baye et al., 2019). Peer tutoring (see page 45) may provide individualised practice for tutees (such as in reading or mathematics) for a whole class at a time. Small-group tuition may be more efficient for supporting up to four pupils at a time. Using digital technologies may be a helpful way to support effective and motivated individual practice if you have a programme at the right level.

Unexpected finding

One-to-two tuition can be as effective as one-to-one tuition but at half the cost. In studies that compare one-to-one and small-group tuition, there is often very little difference between the progress made when intensive teaching is provided in pairs. As the group size gets bigger (one-to-three and one-to-four), progress is not so rapid, but you can support more pupils. It's therefore important to balance the cost and benefit of this approach.

The waves of intervention model can help with planning for extra support. The goal is that all pupils succeed with inclusive quality first teaching for all (Wave 1). To enable all children to keep up, extra interventions in groups may be needed (Wave 2). Any additional intensive and individualised interventions (Wave 3) may be needed for some pupils falling behind. However, these are expensive both in terms of time and cost, and risk the pupil missing out on other teaching, so must be used wisely.

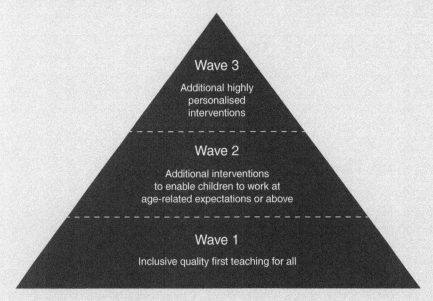

Wave 3

Additional highly
personalised
interventions

Wave 2

Additional interventions
to enable children to work at
age-related expectations or above

Wave 1

Inclusive quality first teaching for all

Figure 2 Waves of intervention model

Teaching tips

✓ When planning one-to-one support, set clear targets over a fixed period of time. Little and often is best, ideally three to four times a week for 20 to 30 minutes for four to six weeks. If you don't see progress after a couple of weeks, you should review and decide whether to change the strategy. If your one-to-one tuition is being led by a teaching assistant then make sure there is time for liaison with you on a regular basis.

✓ Plan a strategy for reintegration. It's often the case that a period of more intensive support helps a pupil catch up, but when they are back with the class they are back where they did not succeed. What will be different now?

✓ Link one-to-one support with classroom teaching. This is important for private tutoring outside school hours. It's important to complement not contradict core teaching.

✓ Be clear about what they might miss. This is a real challenge. Will they miss a normal lesson? If so, they will need to make even more progress in the one-to-one sessions to catch up. Will they miss a different lesson each time? If so, which one? Is it always the same lesson? Are you sure it is not their favourite? Will they fall behind with something else? Can the one-to-one be extra?

✓ Check for progress early on and if it is not working try something else. Be clear about what progress you are expecting and what counts as success.

Leadership tips

✓ Ensure staff are trained in one-to-one strategies. You may think one-to-one teaching is easy, but the relationship with the pupil is crucial. There are only two of you so there is nowhere to hide, for either of you. It can be stressful for pupils to be taught on their own. Maintaining pace and challenge without creating too much frustration is a fine balance and both teachers and teaching assistants will benefit from extra training and support.

✓ Review the cost effectiveness of one-to-one tuition regularly. Large amounts of one-to-one support are expensive in terms of teacher or TA time. If a large number of pupils need one-to-one catch-up support, this needs to be addressed earlier. Intensive small-group support or greater use of individualised support (see page 29) may help avoid pupils falling too far behind. A qualified teacher gets more progress than a TA using the same programme or approach. One-to-two support halves any extra staff costs and doubles the number of children who can be taught.

✓ Build staff capacity for intensive support. A subject leader being given time for intensive one-to-one teaching in mathematics or reading for half a day a week one term is an excellent opportunity for professional learning in precise diagnosis and addressing specific learning needs. Sending TAs on a training course may seem expensive, but, once trained, they will be able to work with a large number of pupils over the next two years.

KEY READINGS

Academic

Baye, A., Inns, A., Lake, C. and Slavin, R. E. (2019), 'A synthesis of quantitative research on reading programs for secondary students', *Reading Research Quarterly*, 54, (2), 133–166.

Pellegrini, M., Lake, C., Inns, A. and Slavin, R. E. (2018), 'Effective programs in elementary mathematics: A best-evidence synthesis', *Best Evidence Encyclopedia*, www.bestevidence.org/word/elem_math_Oct_8_2018.pdf

Practical

Clay, M. M. (2007), *Literacy Lessons Designed for Individuals Part One: Why? When? and How?: Why? When? and How Pt. 1*. London: Heinemann.

Drabble, C. (2016), *Bloomsbury CPD Library: Supporting Children with Special Educational Needs and Disabilities*. London: Bloomsbury Education.

5 THINKING FOR YOURSELF

SELF-REGULATION AND METACOGNITION

Attainment gain	+ 7 months	
Learning benefits	• Helps to motivate learners and instil persistence and resilience in their learning, boosting confidence. • Enables pupils to regulate their emotions and behaviour.	
Unexpected finding	• Low attainers often benefit more from self-regulation and metacognition than their peers.	
Teaching tips	• Choose tasks at the right level of challenge. • Remind learners about what they know and can do. • Teach and demonstrate strategies for the task. • Practise the strategy as a class. • Encourage learners to reflect on the strategy.	
Leadership tips	• It's easy to think you are doing it, but the devil is in the detail. • Plan professional development for staff to learn metacognition and self-regulation in their classrooms. • Ensure strategies are taught for basic thinking and more complex tasks. • Check your approach to assessment includes feedback about the use of strategies.	
Principles	• Goldilocks • The Matthew Effect	

WHAT IS IT?

Self-regulation and metacognition are all about taking responsibility for your own learning. It is like training for a sport such as running. Motivation is key for athletes – how do you motivate yourself to train? What gets you out of bed in the morning? Then there are the feelings about running – how much do you enjoy it? How do you keep training when it is challenging? How do you overcome the tiredness and sore muscles? Finally, there are the different types of running. The techniques for sprinting and the training you need to succeed are different from preparing for a marathon or even a ten-kilometre run.

Self-regulation covers everything: the motivation, managing your feelings and the different strategies and techniques you use to prepare and race. These final areas of strategies and techniques for self-regulation are about managing your thinking or cognition. Strategic planning, monitoring and evaluating your own training are the metacognitive aspects of self-regulation. You are thinking about your own thinking.

DOES IT WORK?

Metacognition and self-regulation approaches have high levels of impact, with classes of pupils making an average of seven months' extra progress over the course of a year. These strategies are more effective when taught in collaborative groups so learners can support each other and make their thinking explicit through discussion. The potential impact of these approaches is high, but can be difficult to achieve in practice as they require pupils to take greater responsibility for their learning and develop their understanding of what is required to succeed. The evidence indicates that teaching these strategies can be effective for low-achieving and older pupils. Harnessing the learner's own awareness and getting them to take responsibility for aspects of their own learning is a bit like finding the Holy Grail of teaching.

Learning benefits

There are important benefits in terms of motivation where learners take responsibility for their learning. Without this basic motivation to succeed learners will not want to spend energy in thinking at all. This willingness to try helps to develop persistence and resilience through learning how to be strategic. Developing a repertoire of successful techniques and strategies also encourages the learner to choose and commit to a particular approach to make it work for them. As learners take greater responsibility and become more confident they are more able to take control of their emotions and to manage their feelings and their own motivation. This is where metacognition can lead to greater overall self-regulation.

HOW DOES IT WORK?

Whenever we tackle any learning task or activity, we have some metacognitive knowledge about:

- **ourselves as a learner:** our own abilities and attitudes
- **strategies:** what strategies we think are effective and applicable
- **the task:** the particular type of activity we are tackling.

In every learning task, we start with this knowledge, then apply and adapt it. This is metacognitive regulation. It is about planning how to undertake a task, working on it while monitoring the strategy to check progress, then evaluating the overall success. When the learner is in control of the task, they progress more efficiently than when they are being prompted or supported through a task.

As learners work through tasks they apply their own metacognitive and cognitive skills, and update their metacognitive knowledge (of themselves, of appropriate strategies and about tasks), as well as updating their subject knowledge and skills. Taking responsibility for planning, monitoring and evaluating becomes a habit and the teacher can focus on helping learners in being more strategic, rather than directing every step.

As well as explicit instruction and modelling, classroom dialogue and discussion can be used to develop metacognitive skills. Peer-to-peer and pupil-teacher talk can help to build knowledge and understanding of cognitive and metacognitive strategies. This might be through think-alouds or short structured work in pairs to plan, monitor and evaluate tasks. However, this kind of talk or dialogue needs to be purposeful and practised a lot, with teachers guiding and supporting the interaction to ensure it is challenging and builds on prior subject knowledge.

> '**Study skills really aren't the point. Learning is about one's relationship with oneself and one's ability to exert the effort, self-control, and critical self-assessment necessary to achieve the best possible results – and about overcoming risk aversion, failure, distractions, and sheer laziness in pursuit of REAL achievement. This is self-regulated learning.**'
>
> Linda Nilson (2013)

 ## Principles

Principle 1: Goldilocks

The devil is in the detail in teaching for self-regulation and metacognition. You've got to get the level of challenge right for the learners and have a good match with your subject and curriculum content. It's easy to miss this 'sweet spot'. Too hard and pupils will not be able to think metacognitively; too easy a task and they won't need to.

Principle 2: The Matthew Effect

Metacognitive approaches often help lower-attaining pupils more than those who are usually successful. This is for two reasons. First, high attainers work out strategies for themselves, and second, they find tasks easier so don't always need to use strategies.

Unexpected findings

Learners have different self-regulation capabilities in different subjects. Don't assume that just because a pupil is strategic and metacognitive in reading, they will be in mathematics, or even writing. Also, how you think and how you feel are inseparable for learners. If a pupil lacks confidence this will affect their ability to be metacognitive. Any anxiety will reduce their capability to be strategic or reflective.

Teaching tips

✓ Choose tasks at the right level of challenge. Too hard and pupils will not be able to think metacognitively; too easy a task and they won't need to.

✓ Remind learners about what they know and can do in relation to a new task.

✓ Explicitly teach self-regulation and metacognition strategies appropriate for the task.

✓ Demonstrate and model each new strategy.

✓ Practise each strategy as a class, in a group and individually (with guided and independent practice).

✓ Encourage learners to reflect on how appropriate the strategy was, how successfully they applied it, and where they might use it again or how they might adapt it.

Leadership tips

✓ Plan continuing professional development for staff to learn about and to develop metacognition and self-regulation in their classrooms. This should consider in detail how they can match the strategies to the specific curriculum content being taught.

✓ Plan for the time to develop and apply these approaches in the classroom with the whole staff. The challenge is to make the strategies specific to the learning in each area of the curriculum. Consider setting up small groups to look at different subjects or ages, and then ask them to report back to the whole staff.

✓ Make sure strategies are taught for basic thinking, such as techniques for memorisation, as well as for more complex thinking such as problem-solving approaches in mathematics.

✓ Check your approach to assessment and recording includes feedback about the use of strategies and the development of learners' self-regulation.

KEY READINGS

Academic

EEF (2018), 'Metacognition and self-regulation', *Sutton Trust-EEF Teaching and Learning Toolkit*, https://educationendowmentfoundation.org.uk/resources/teaching-learning-toolkit/meta-cognition-and-self-regulation

Quigley, A., Muijs, D. and Stringer, E. (2018), 'Metacognition and self-regulated learning: Guidance report', https://educationendowmentfoundation.org.uk/tools/guidance-reports/metacognition-and-self-regulated-learning/

Zimmerman, B. J. (1990), 'Self-regulated learning and academic achievement: An overview', *Educational Psychologist*, 25, (1), 3–17.

Practical

Fogarty, R. and Pete, B. (2018), *Metacognition: The neglected skill set for empowering students*. Cheltenham, Victoria: Hawker Brownlow Education.

6 SPEAKING AND LISTENING SKILLS

⬆	**Attainment gain**	+ 5 months	-1 0 +1 +2 +3 +4 **+5** +6 +7 +8
	Learning benefits	• Improved behaviour and social outcomes. • Increased learner confidence.	
❗	**Unexpected finding**	• Speaking and listening activities reveal pupils' learning and knowledge gaps.	
💡	**Teaching tips**	• Teach pupils to work in groups and to participate in speaking and listening activities. • Make sure the task matches the learning outcomes. • Use your observations of pupils' talk to evaluate how well they have mastered new concepts and vocabulary.	
👆	**Leadership tips**	• Ensure your assessment approach values speaking and listening activities. • Develop a common core of collaborative learning structures and types of activities.	
🔧	**Principles**	• Goldilocks	

WHAT IS IT?

Speaking and listening approaches emphasise the importance of spoken language and verbal interaction in the classroom. They are based on the idea that comprehension and reading skills benefit from explicit discussion of either the content or processes of learning – or both. For older learners this can support their written language too (Littleton and Mercer, 2013). The aim is to put listening and speaking at the centre of classroom learning.

DOES IT WORK?

It's easy to forget, as pupils get older, that they still need to articulate their thinking and understanding. Opportunities to use new vocabulary are essential if new language is to become part of the way they think and express their ideas. This idea of introducing new ideas and new vocabulary, then providing opportunities for learners to practise and become familiar with it, before expecting formal written work, is a useful way of thinking about learning in all subjects of the curriculum (Mercer, 2002).

Learning benefits

Most speaking and listening approaches use collaboration in the classroom through structured group work or activities focussing on verbal interaction and communication. These have direct benefits on language capability and reasoning (Murphy et al., 2009). Research reports that wider aspects of learning, such as classroom climate and behaviour, improve when these approaches are adopted (Tolmie et al., 2010).

HOW DOES IT WORK?

Listening and speaking is at the core of academic learning. New knowledge and new vocabulary extend our understanding of different subjects as we learn. We tend to focus in schools on listening as the main approach to teach new content. However, it is also vital that pupils use this information for it to become part of their language repertoire.

As pupils practise articulating their thinking and ideas in activities planned to develop subject knowledge and understanding, they use new concepts and vocabulary. It is a bit like learning a foreign language. It's all very well understanding what is said to you, but until you can express your own thoughts you haven't mastered the language. Subject learning is no different. If you never use technical vocabulary from geography or science when speaking, how will you be able to compose written sentences with these ideas?

Principles

Principle 1: Goldilocks

Planning effective discussion or speaking activities isn't straightforward. It is easy to waste time in explanations or in overly complex tasks. At the same time unfocussed discussion isn't productive. Pupils need practice in talking together and in listening to each other. Structured activities are often an easier place to start (see collaborative learning, page 109). Be clear about what you want the class to talk about and what kinds of language you are expecting them to use, for example richer descriptions or more coherent argumentation and reasoning. Evaluate informally to check the activities are successful. Some adjustment and practice is likely to be needed.

Unexpected finding

Teachers often report that hearing their pupils talk about learning tasks and content helps them identify capabilities in some pupils they didn't realise they had, and gaps in knowledge and understanding they had missed. It is a valuable assessment opportunity to hear learners' 'productive' language capability about a particular topic or aspect of the curriculum. This is the language they use spontaneously themselves to communicate. It is surprising how often you are convinced pupils understand ideas or vocabulary, but struggle to articulate it clearly when speaking. Assessment can be undertaken informally and quickly as you monitor a group activity by eavesdropping into their discussions.

Teaching tips

✓ Teach pupils to work in groups and to participate in speaking and listening activities like 'show and tell' for younger children or debating for older learners.

✓ Make sure the task matches the learning outcomes.

✓ Use your observations of pupils' talk to evaluate how well they have mastered new concepts and vocabulary.

Leadership tips

✓ Ensure your planning and assessment approach values speaking and listening activities and teachers' observations of these. Do not require teachers to record yet more tracking of progress.

✓ Develop a common core of collaborative learning tasks, structures and types of activities across the school that teachers can draw on. Some are easy to use with any age groups, such as 'think, pair, share'. Others, particularly those where pupils take on specific roles, need more explanation and practice. How will you ensure progression?

✓ Be careful some activities don't get overused. If you have staff development on different techniques, pupils may experience the same activity in lots of different lessons. Some kinds of activities have something like a half-life. They get overused and decay quickly. Others last for longer, but can still be used too frequently and both teachers and pupils become jaded.

KEY READINGS

. . . .

Practical

Alexander, R. (2012), 'Dialogic teaching', www.robinalexander.org.uk/
dialogic-teaching

EEF (2018), 'Oral language interventions', *Sutton Trust-EEF Teaching and Learning Toolkit*, https://educationendowmentfoundation.org.uk/evidence-summaries/
teaching-learning-toolkit/oral-language-interventions

University of Cambridge, 'Thinking together', https://thinkingtogether.educ.cam.
ac.uk (a project led by Neil Mercer)

7 PEER TUTORING

Attainment gain	+ 5 months	

Learning benefits	• Greater confidence in subjects and more positive attitudes towards learning. • Improved self-esteem. • Improved social interaction and classroom behaviour.
Unexpected finding	• Same-sex pairing works best.
Teaching tips	• Trial peer tutoring in short, termly bursts – lasting ten or fewer weeks. • Take time to prepare. • Model questioning and feedback for pupil tutors. • Differentiate materials and question prompts for different attainment levels. • Monitor and help lower-achieving pairs. • Use this approach for consolidation and practice.
Leadership tips	• Frame peer tutoring as an opportunity for cross-class, collaborative professional development. • Give teachers time to prepare. • Check the level of challenge of tasks and the pace of tutoring sessions. • Allay parents' fears about their children being taught by (or teaching) other pupils. • Try rewards such as book vouchers.
Principles	• Bananarama • Goldilocks • The Matthew Effect

WHAT IS IT?

Peer tutoring enables pupils to teach each other, working in pairs or small groups. The teacher becomes 'guide from the side' rather than 'sage from the stage'. This is an opportunity for you to step back from whole-class instruction to guide pupils on how to teach their peers about specific problems. Pupil tutors are empowered to give feedback to their fellow pupils, explaining, demonstrating, correcting and praising their tutees.

There are three different types of peer tutoring: cross-age tutoring, reciprocal tutoring and peer-assisted learning. In cross-age tutoring, an older pupil acts as a tutor for a younger tutee or tutees. In reciprocal tutoring, pupils (usually in the same year group) take it in turns to be tutor and tutee. Most cross-age and reciprocal tutoring programmes include detailed instructions for the training and delivery of the programme. In peer-assisted learning, tutors work with tutees for 25–35 minutes two or three times a week on specific maths problems or reading challenges.

DOES IT WORK?

Introducing peer tutoring adds an extra four to five months' learning gain for pupils during an academic year. While both tutors and tutees benefit, the gains are often greater for tutors. In cross-age tutoring, lower-attaining peers may benefit more (Leung, 2018).

Peer tutoring is effective in mathematics (for a range of skills) and reading (including oral reading and comprehension). Impact has been observed in physical education, with smaller effects in arts, science and technology, psychology, and languages.

The evidence is strong but recent trials in England yielded no extra impact on attainment compared with teaching as usual (Lloyd et al., 2015a and 2015b). This may be because peer tutoring is less powerful in schools where collaborative learning is already commonplace. It's a low-cost intervention, but don't underestimate the time needed for training and preparation.

Peer tutoring is mostly undertaken in primary schools. Yet the evidence suggests it could have the greatest impact for secondary school pupils and for college and university students (Leung, 2018). We need more trials of programmes deploying university students as tutors to help sixth formers in their study in order to explore the effects of this further.

Learning benefits

Peer tutoring can have many other benefits besides attainment gains. Pupils can develop more positive attitudes to the subjects being tutored. If delivered well, it can boost the self-esteem of tutors and tutees. Teachers using a maths tutoring programme reported that pupils gained confidence in maths; they also believed it developed problem-solving and social skills, although the study was unable to substantiate these claims (Lloyd et al., 2015b). Teachers report that cross-age peer tutoring can create social and supportive bonds between pupils from different year groups.

Peer tutoring also offers welcome relief from being in front of the class, both for the teacher and for the pupils. Remember, variety is the spice of learning. Variety is successful when it improves engagement and allows a faster pace or greater challenge in learning.

HOW DOES IT WORK?

Pupils acting as tutors have to think hard about a topic, explain it clearly and help their tutee when they get stuck. This helps them overcome common mistakes. Tutees respond well to working with an older peer. It may be through improved social–emotional skills and behaviour that peer tutoring makes achievement gains possible or it could be down to the direct instruction and practice delivered in a successful lesson.

> 'It would be a mistake to think of peer tutoring as an easy option.'
>
> Allen Thurston and Maria Cockerill (2017)

 ## Principles

Principle 1: Bananarama

Structured peer tutoring programmes that offer detailed instructional guidance on what to do but also allow space for teacher and student creativity have yielded higher levels of intrinsic motivation, curiosity and self-worth among pupils than either rigid or unstructured formats. Striking the optimal balance is easier said than done. Teachers bought into the concept of peer tutoring in a trial of paired reading in secondary schools (Lloyd et al., 2015a), but many struggled to follow what was seen as an overly prescribed approach of the programme. One of the tensions was about the content of lessons and activities to ensure all pupils were challenged.

> 'It has been a bit of a struggle to get resources together... pitching questions at the right level [for tutors and tutees], making sure there's going to be enough questions, finding different questions each week'
>
> A teacher in the EEF trial of Shared Maths (Lloyd et al., 2015b)

Principle 2: Goldilocks

It is important to get the level of challenge just right in peer tutoring programmes. In cross-age tutoring, the maths questions or reading material should be above the independent level of the tutee, but below that of the tutor. Teachers can also model effective praise for tutors: not too much, not too little, and focussed on the learning task itself.

Principle 3: The Matthew Effect

Peer tutoring can benefit the highest achievers in the classroom the most. Pupils acting as tutees who are already top of the class experience greater gains than their lower-ranked peers. However, peer-to-peer learning can still boost the progress of pupils who need most support in the classroom: low-achieving pupils,

pupils from low-income backgrounds, and those with special educational needs or English as an additional language. Low-achieving pupils acting as tutors, for example, experience larger gains than their higher-performing peers (Leung, 2018).

The results are different when it comes to cross-age tutoring, however. Teachers recently found low-achieving pupils struggled as tutors *and* tutees in two major trials of cross-age peer tutoring. In one trial, 13-year-old tutors taught 11-year-olds in maths problems (Lloyd et al., 2015b). In another, ten-year-olds taught eight-year-olds in reading (Lloyd et al., 2015a). In both trials, some low-achieving tutors suffered a blow to their self-esteem when they realised they lagged behind pupils who were two years younger than them. Other low-achieving pairs failed to make progress, as they were unable to grasp the content, corrections or praise required for genuine learning to take place. Teachers felt there was a lack of guidance and time for tutoring to work for such pupils, indicating again how important it is to be careful about how peer tutoring is implemented.

Unexpected finding

Same-sex tutor pairs are more effective than mixed-sex pairs, regardless of whether the tutor is male or female. This may be because pupils are already preoccupied with their stereotyped gender roles, which distracts them from learning. It is possible some female tutors may feel uncomfortable with their position of authority, while some male tutees may feel uneasy being placed in a subordinate role (Leung, 2018).

Teaching tips

✓ Less is more. Peer tutoring works best in short termly bursts – lasting ten or fewer weeks. One review found twice the impact on learning for interventions less than four weeks in duration (Cohen et al., 1982). Received wisdom is for sessions to last no more than 30 minutes and tutor training sessions to last no more than 45 minutes. In a trial of a 16-week paired reading programme, one teacher reported that students got bored (Lloyd et al., 2015a).

✓ Brevity, however, has to be balanced against the need for proper preparation, without which peer tutoring is rendered ineffective – particularly for learners who need extra attention. Teachers report it takes ten weeks to get ten-year-olds to a point where they are teaching rather than telling their tutees what to do (Lloyd et al., 2015a).

✓ Model questioning and feedback for pupil tutors so their peer interaction moves learning on. This requires the process to be broken down into manageable chunks for pupils (and teachers), and for sessions to be structured by using questioning frames or prompt cards, as well as providing detailed training and feedback for tutors.

✓ Develop easier and harder materials and question prompts for pairs with different attainment levels.

✓ Use teacher and teaching assistant support to focus help for lower-achieving pairs.

✓ Use peer tutoring for consolidation and practice. Peer tutoring works best when it consolidates learning in the classroom. Discuss with tutors the questions (and answers) you will be working on at the end of a lesson to build confidence ahead of a peer tutoring session. Tutees can explain to tutors what they have been doing in recent lessons. The sessions should supplement normal teaching, rather than replacing it.

✓ Try randomly partnering tutees and tutors. Pupils won't feel demoralised for being paired with lower achievers, and you may be pleasantly surprised by the results.

Leadership tips

✓ Use peer tutoring as an opportunity for cross-class, collaborative professional development focussed on research. In cross-age peer tutoring, some studies have found a two-year age gap is the optimal age difference between tutors and tutees. Tutors are sufficiently older to be respected by their younger peers but near enough in age to be relatable to. We don't know whether this two-year rule holds for teenagers and young adults as it does for younger children. We suspect the optimal age gap at this level relates to subject knowledge and understanding. Too big a gap and the tutor does not benefit; too small a gap and the tutor cannot see how to help the tutee. Ask a group of teachers to lead a research project to find the optimal age difference in your context as part of their professional development.

✓ Teachers need time to think through what is needed to make any intervention work. In this instance, they must consider how difficult materials for tutoring pairs should be, the intensity of training required for tutors, and the management of the classroom when pupils are organised into pairs. Only then will they realise the promise of peer tutoring. Make sure your teachers have time to consider all these different aspects before they begin a peer tutoring programme.

✓ Check the level of challenge of the tasks and the pace of tutoring sessions when teachers begin implementing them.

✓ Allay parents' fears about their children being taught (or teaching) other pupils. Explaining the programme and its potential benefits to parents can be a useful component of peer tutoring. It can help to address concerns that teachers are abrogating their professional responsibilities. Use some of the research studies discussed in this book to back up your arguments if you feel this would help.

✓ Offer rewards to pupils who tutor. Studies in which tangible items were used as rewards, such as 'golden time' or book vouchers, displayed nearly twice the impact than those involving points as rewards. Encouraging competition among pairs or teams of pupils didn't work (Leung, 2018).

KEY READINGS

Academic

Leung, K. C. (2019), 'An updated meta-analysis on the effect of peer tutoring on tutors' achievement', *School Psychology International*, 40, (2), 200–214.

Lloyd, C., Edovald, T., Kiss, Z., Skipp, A., Morris, S. and Ahmed, H. (2015), 'Paired reading evaluation report and executive summary'. London: EEF.

Lloyd, C., Edovald, T., Kiss, Z., Skipp, A., Morris, S. and Ahmed, H. (2015), 'Durham shared maths project: Evaluation report and executive summary'. London: EEF.

Tymms, P., Merrell, C., Thurston, A., Andor, J., Topping, K. and Miller, D. (2011), 'Improving attainment across a whole district: School reform through peer tutoring in a randomized controlled trial', *School Effectiveness and School Improvement*, 22, (3), 265–289.

Practical

Kelly, B., 'Peer and cross age tutoring'. Olympia, WA: Washington Office of Superintendent of Public Instruction. http://radschwartzfoundation.com/wp-content/uploads/Misc/Bucket%201%20The%20Peer%20Tutoring%20Resource%20Library/In%20your%20classroom/Lesson%20plans%20and%20tools/Guide%20to%20Peer%20and%20Cross-age%20Tutoring_Washington%20Reading%20Corps.pdf

Thurston, A. and Cockerill, M. (2017), *Peer Tutoring in Schools* (5th edn.). Belfast: Queen's University Belfast, https://pure.qub.ac.uk/portal/files/130755742/PairedReadingManual_v5.doc

8 MASTERY LEARNING

 Attainment gain | + 5 months |

 Learning benefits
- Builds growth mindset.
- All learners succeed in key curriculum objectives.

! Unexpected finding
- Mastery learning can help close the attainment gap.

Teaching tips
- Target the use of mastery learning for specific objectives.
- Plan catch-up and keep-up activities.
- Don't move on until everyone has achieved 'mastery'.

Leadership tips
- Change your curriculum and lesson planning approach to embed mastery.
- Agree 'mastery' criteria as a staff – then stick to them!
- Provide a structure for 'keep-up' support.

Principles
- The Matthew Effect
- Bananarama

WHAT IS IT?

In mastery learning, the curriculum only goes as fast as pupils learn. Traditional teaching keeps time spent on a topic constant and allows pupils' 'mastery' of curriculum content to vary. Mastery learning keeps learning outcomes constant – everyone learns everything – but the approach varies the time needed for pupils to become proficient in these objectives. Some people are uncomfortable with the term 'mastery' due to its masculine connotations.

Mastery learning breaks subject matter and learning content into units with specified objectives that are taught until they are achieved. In this it is similar to direct instruction (see page 54). Learners work through each block of content in a series of sequential steps and must demonstrate a high level of success on tests, getting at least 80 per cent right, before progressing to the next unit. Those who do not reach the required level are provided with extra tuition, peer support, small-group teaching or homework, so they can reach the expected level.

Some of the ideas behind mastery learning date back to American schools in the 1920s and the work of Carleton Washburne who developed the 'Winnetka Plan' in Illinois in the USA (Block, 1971). This approach used tests for the curriculum basics (specifically multiple choice and fill-in items) with detailed self-instruction booklets and self-correction exercises. Pupils proceeded at their own rates until mastery was demonstrated subject by subject for half the school day. This individual mastery approach was then supplemented with group work and social and creative cross-curricular activities using drama, projects and student reports for the rest of the day. A version of mastery learning was revived in programmed instruction in the late 1950s based on the work of B. F. Skinner (1938). It aimed to provide students with instructional materials to move at their own pace and receive constant feedback (see also individualised instruction, page 103). During the 1960s, Benjamin Bloom's 'Learning for Mastery' led to a resurgence of interest (Bloom, 1968). He is acknowledged as the originator of the mastery model. Bloom argued learners would not spend more time overall on activities to achieve proficiency. Although it may take longer in the early stages, learners would need less time to master more advanced material because of their higher levels of basic competence.

> 'After forty years of intensive research on school learning in the United States as well as abroad, my major conclusion is: What any person in the world can learn, almost all persons can learn if provided with appropriate prior and current conditions of learning.'
>
> **Benjamin Bloom**

Several aspects of mastery learning are similar to other contemporary approaches, such as the use of initial diagnostic assessments like universal screening in response-to-intervention models (Guskey and Jung, 2011). Formative assessments and tests to monitor pupils' progress give detailed feedback on what they need to do to close the gap between their current performance and the desired goal. It's similar to assessment for learning and feedback models (Black and Wiliam, 1998; Hattie and Timperley, 2007).

DOES IT WORK?

Several older research reviews indicate mastery learning approaches can be effective, leading to an extra five months' progress (Guskey and Pigott, 1988). These studies show that mastery learning is effective when pupils work in groups or teams and take responsibility for supporting each other's progress (see also collaborative learning, page 109, and peer tutoring, page 45). A high bar should be set for achievement of mastery (80 per cent to 90 per cent on the relevant test). By contrast, the approach appears to be less effective when pupils work at their own pace (see also individualised learning, page 103).

Mastery learning is effective when used as an occasional or extra teaching strategy: programmes of less than 12 weeks report higher impact than longer programmes. Based on this evidence, schools should consider using mastery learning for areas of learning that are hard to consolidate, rather than for all lessons.

However, it is important to note that these older approaches are different from the current definitions of 'teaching for mastery'. Less evidence is available for contemporary versions and recent evaluations have not demonstrated the same benefits (Jerrim et al., 2015). There is less emphasis on testing and ensuring a high level of mastery based on performance in contemporary versions.

Learning benefits

By ensuring everyone succeeds, mastery learning supports a 'growth mindset' (Dweck, 2016) approach where learners are encouraged to believe they can succeed through effort and practice. Mastery makes success for all a key responsibility of the teacher. It is a no-excuses approach. Some learners may need more support, instruction or practice than others, but everyone succeeds or no one moves forward. The curriculum pace is determined by the learning of the class (Bloom, 1980).

> **'Creativity follows mastery, so mastery of skills is the first priority for young talent.'**
>
> **Benjamin Bloom**

HOW DOES IT WORK?

Mastery learning is not a new approach, though different versions have been developed and used at different times. It is based on the belief that all pupils can learn when provided with appropriate activities and support. Learners are provided with regular and specific feedback about their progress. This helps learners identify where they have been successful and where they have been less successful.

Principles

Principle 1: The Matthew Effect

Mastery learning is a promising strategy to close the attainment gap. Low-attaining pupils make more progress from this approach than high-attaining students, according to the *Sutton Trust-EEF Teaching and Learning Toolkit*. Pupils from disadvantaged backgrounds can certainly benefit. Teachers need to plan how to manage the time of pupils who make progress quickly.

Principle 2: Bananarama

The effects of mastery learning tend to cluster at two points; two of the meta-analyses show little or no impact, while the rest show an impact of up to six months' extra progress (EEF, 2015). This variation implies that making mastery learning work is challenging. Setting mastery objectives and criteria are key. What are the non-negotiables in the curriculum everyone must achieve?

> **'Order and simplification are the first steps towards mastery of a subject'**
>
> Thomas Mann

How direct is direct instruction?

Direct instruction is closely related to mastery learning except that the curriculum is precisely specified too. The following principles come from research on direct instruction (Coyne et al., 2009). We don't think most people would recognise these as 'direct instruction'.

Key principles of direct instruction:

- ✓ **Conspicuous strategies:** Explicit teaching of key learning strategies to make them unambiguous and available to all students using clear examples.

- ✓ **Mediated scaffolding:** Characterised by the initial, intentional and temporary support provided to learners by teachers, peers and materials for comprehension instruction.

- ✓ **Strategic integration:** The aim is to build on what pupils already know and can do by explicitly and systematically teaching students to integrate and relate new information, concepts and strategies with previous knowledge and skills so that they can become more adaptable in applying rules and strategies.

- ✓ **Primed background knowledge:** This is what pupils 'bring to the table' and what they use to make meaningful connections with the new concepts, information or strategies they are being taught. Priming, or activating, background knowledge supports strategic integration.

- ✓ **Judicious review:** This involves repeatedly presenting opportunities for learners to apply and develop new knowledge and skills in a careful sequence. Review is considered most effective when it is distributed, cumulative and varied. Review is considered sufficient when a pupil can perform a task automatically and fluently.

Unexpected finding

Several studies indicate that well-executed mastery learning approaches can narrow the gap in achievement for disadvantaged pupils.

Teaching tips

✓ Target your use of mastery learning for specific objectives – mastery learning is a complementary strategy and is not designed to be used all of the time. It aims to consolidate basic skills to a level of mastery or fluency so these skills can be applied and used.

✓ The challenge in mastery learning is how you keep the class moving together. Some pupils will learn more quickly than others so planning activities to help pupils catch up or keep up is essential. This should be done as quickly as possible (ideally the same day or at least in the same week).

✓ Don't move on until everyone has achieved mastery. This is a key principle. If you move some pupils on before everyone has succeeded, you are not doing mastery learning.

Leadership tips

✓ Change your curriculum and lesson planning approach to fit the objectives. Mastery learning requires a challenging restructuring of the curriculum and how it is planned and paced. This will need flexibility in weekly and termly planning as well as access to additional resources.

✓ Agree 'mastery' criteria as a staff – then stick to them! What are the non-negotiable skills and knowledge that will set the 'mastery' criteria for each subject and age group?

✓ Provide a structure for 'keep-up' support. A mastery approach has implications for support and the deployment of teaching assistants in particular. A school-wide approach that supports the achievement of mastery by all pupils is a key ingredient. This could involve the effective deployment of teaching assistants (see page 25), providing teaching time for additional small-group support and staff professional development.

KEY READINGS

Academic

Kulik, C. L. C., Kulik, J. A. and Bangert-Drowns, R. L. (1990), 'Effectiveness of mastery learning programs: A meta-analysis', *Review of Educational Research*, 60, (2), 265–299.

Slavin, R. E. (1987), 'Mastery learning reconsidered', *Review of Educational Research*, 57, (2), 175–213.

Practical

Cain, M. (2018), *Teaching for Mastery in Writing: A strategy for helping children get good at words*. London: Bloomsbury Education.

Dolan, L., Ford, C., Newton, V. and Kellam, S. G. (1989), 'The mastery learning manual', unpublished manual, www.jhsph.edu/research/centers-and-institutes/johns-hopkins-center-for-prevention-and-early-intervention/Publications/mlm.pdf

Drury, H. (2018), *How to Teach Mathematics for Mastery*. Oxford: Oxford University Press.

Guskey, T. R. (2010), 'Lessons of mastery learning', *Educational Leadership*, 68, (2), 52–57, www.ascd.org/publications/educational-leadership/oct10/vol68/num02/Lessons-of-Mastery-Learning.aspx

McCourt, M. (2019), *Teaching for Mastery*. Woodbridge: John Catt Educational.

9 PHONICS

Attainment gain	+ 4 months	

Learning benefits
- Improves fluency in decoding.
- Builds skills necessary for comprehension.
- Can build self-confidence in the learner's capability.

 Unexpected finding
- We don't know how effective phonics is for successful readers.

Teaching tips
- Little and often is best.
- Check for understanding.
- Monitor progress and adapt your pace.
- Link reading and spelling.
- Keep it interesting!

 Leadership tips
- Check teacher knowledge.
- Develop a consistent whole-school approach to phonics.
- Ensure efficiency.

Principles
- Bananarama
- Goldilocks
- Threshold Effect

WHAT IS IT?

Phonics is an approach to teaching reading, and some aspects of writing, which focusses on developing learners' phonemic awareness skills and decoding fluency. This involves hearing, identifying and using phonemes or sound patterns in English. The aim is to teach learners the relationship between these sounds and the written spelling patterns, or graphemes,

> **'Fluent, accurate decoding is a hallmark of skilled reading'**
> **Moats (1998)**

which represent them. Phonics emphasises the skills of decoding new words by sounding them out and combining or 'blending' the sound-spelling patterns to develop automaticity and fluency.

Synthetic phonics emphasises building fluency by putting single sounds or phonemes together, such as /k, æ, t/ to make 'cat' (synthesis). Analytic phonics emphasises patterns in the sounds of single or combinations of letters (phonograms), such as in 'that, than, then, them' or b-at, f-at, h-at, m-at (rime).

DOES IT WORK?

Phonics approaches are effective in supporting younger readers to master some of the basic skills of reading, with an average impact of an extra four months' progress reported in the *Sutton Trust-EEF Teaching and Learning Toolkit*. Research suggests phonics is beneficial for younger learners (four- to seven-year-olds) as they begin to read and as a catch-up approach for those who struggle. Teaching phonics is more effective on average than other approaches to early reading (such as whole language or alphabetic approaches), but effective phonics techniques are usually embedded in a rich literacy environment for early readers and are just one part of a literacy strategy (Torgerson et al., 2019).

> **'For many children, practising the ability to recognize sounds in words can make a big difference in how fast they learn to read'**
>
> Kimberly Oliver Burnim (2012), US National Teacher of the Year in 2006

For older readers who are still struggling to develop reading skills, phonics approaches may be less successful than other approaches such as reading comprehension strategies (see page 63) and metacognition and self-regulation (see page 35). The difference may indicate children aged ten or above who haven't succeeded using phonics approaches require a different approach. Students may have other difficulties related to vocabulary and comprehension that phonics doesn't target. Learning how to read words you don't understand has limited value. Older learners who continue to struggle may also have other specific language needs that need to be met.

Qualified teachers are up to twice as effective as other staff in getting results from phonics interventions, indicating a secure knowledge of phonics and teaching expertise are key to successful teaching of early reading.

Learning benefits

Fluency in decoding is an important skill. For readers who are struggling to progress, improving their decoding capability is likely to help. This may then build their confidence so they can tackle more challenging texts. The aim is to build capability and confidence to improve overall fluency. Once words can be decoded fluently the learner can think about meaning and making sense of what they read.

> **'Is speed of barking at print what we mean by reading fluency?'**
>
> S. Jay Samuels (2007)

HOW DOES IT WORK?

Phonics builds up fluency in decoding, so learners can think about the meaning of what they read, rather than trying to work out what the text says. The idea is that if you can build up fluent and automatic word reading skills then this frees up working memory to focus on meaning. There needs to be a balance in emphasis between decoding and comprehension, but in the early stages it is important to develop rapid and efficient decoding skills.

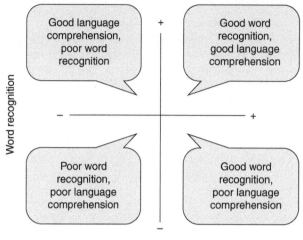

Figure 3 The simple view of reading – ensure an effective balance

 Principles

Principle 1: Bananarama

Most teachers and schools use some phonics in their teaching. There are a range of different approaches and the evidence doesn't support one technique over another. You should choose a consistent approach to sounding out and blending, particularly in the way letters are pronounced.

Principle 2: Goldilocks

It is easy to spend too much time going over activities that the children either can already do or are struggling to master. Regular informal observation and assessment will help to target what children can do, where they need more practice and what new steps they should take next.

Principle 3: Threshold Effect

How much phonics is enough? The evidence suggests that short bursts with frequent repetition until fluency is retained is the best approach (Sobel et al., 2011). More is not necessarily better. Effective assessment and diagnosis are vital here. Don't teach it if they already can do it. It's a waste of your and your pupils' time.

Unexpected finding

The evidence on the effectiveness of phonics is mainly from studies of children and young people who are struggling to learn to read. It is therefore proven to be effective for catch up but it's no panacea. We don't know how much phonics successful readers need and we don't know how useful extra phonics is when a reader has failed with a phonics-based approach.

Teaching tips

✓ Make sure you keep phonics lessons interesting and challenging for learners. Little and often is better than long sessions, which become routine.

✓ Make sure children understand the words they can read. Some children will struggle with wider aspects of language capability, which will need to be addressed.

✓ Monitor progress so you can change pace frequently. What can you skip or accelerate? What requires more consolidation?

✓ Link spelling and writing with your phonics teaching. Ensure children practise writing the word they can read. This will help embed common phonic patterns.

✓ Some children will need lots of motivated practice to become fluent. This will need extra time so they can get further support.

Leadership tips

✓ Ensure all teachers of early reading have a good grounding in phonics and that new teachers are up to speed with how early reading should be taught. Teachers' phonological and phonemic knowledge is usually sufficient, but for many their understanding of phonic and morphological constructs and terminology is weak.

✓ Adopt a consistent approach to phonics instruction across the school so children know what is expected (for example in pronunciation and blending).

✓ Ensure the teaching of phonics is efficient. The balance between being systematic and efficient is a challenging one to strike.

✓ Phonics is a means to an end. Fluent decoding is essential in learning to read but comprehension is the final goal.

KEY READINGS

Practical

EEF (2018), 'Preparing for literacy: Improving communication, language and literacy in the early years: Guidance report', https://educationendowmentfoundation.org.uk/tools/guidance-reports/preparing-for-literacy/

Higgins, S., Henderson, P., Martell, T., Sharples, J. and Waugh, D. (2017), 'Improving literacy In Key Stage 1: Guidance report'. London: EEF, https://educationendowmentfoundation.org.uk/tools/guidance-reports/literacy-ks-1

Snowling, M. J. and Hulme, C. (2007), *The Science of Reading: A handbook.* London: Wiley Blackwell.

10 UNDERSTANDING TEXTS

TEACHING READING COMPREHENSION STRATEGIES

 Attainment gain +6 months

 Learning benefits
- Improves confidence in reading.
- Provides access to the wider curriculum.
- Develops vocabulary.

 Unexpected finding
- Digital technology can be useful for reading comprehension.

 Teaching tips
- Get the level of challenge right.
- Don't get stuck in a rut.
- Diagnose difficulties.
- Teach for transfer.

 Leadership tips
- Develop teachers' knowledge of reading comprehension strategies through CPD.
- Plan a progression of strategy use to help the learner to use the strategies they need for different types of texts.

 Principles
- Goldilocks
- Bananarama

WHAT IS IT?

The explicit teaching of reading comprehension strategies focusses on the learners' understanding of written text. Pupils are taught a range of techniques and approaches that enable them to understand the meaning of what they read. These include approaches such as inferring meaning from context; summarising or identifying key points; using graphic or semantic organisers to represent ideas on paper; developing questioning strategies; monitoring their own comprehension and identifying difficulties themselves (see also self-regulation and metacognition, page 35, and developing decoding fluency, page 57).

DOES IT WORK?

On average, the explicit teaching of reading comprehension approaches can deliver an extra six months' progress. Successful reading comprehension approaches allow activities to be tailored to pupils' current reading capabilities, and involve activities and texts that provide an effective, but not overwhelming, challenge.

Many of the approaches can be combined with collaborative learning techniques (see page 109) and phonics (see page 57) to develop reading skills. The use of techniques such as graphic organisers and drawing pupils' attention to text features are particularly useful when reading expository or information texts.

Comparative findings indicate reading comprehension approaches are more effective than phonics or oral language approaches for upper primary and secondary pupils, for both short-term and long-term impact. However, supporting struggling readers requires a coordinated effort across the curriculum and a mix of approaches. No particular strategy should be seen as a panacea, and careful diagnosis of the reasons why an individual pupil is struggling should guide the choice of intervention strategies.

> 'Were all instructors to realize that the quality of mental process, not the production of correct answers, is the measure of educative growth something hardly less than a revolution in teaching would be worked.'
>
> John Dewey (1916)

 ## Learning benefits

Teaching reading comprehension strategies boosts confidence in reading and helps to develop vocabulary. As reading is a key skill across the curriculum, this helps pupils to access other subjects, not just English.

> 'The development of language is part of the development of the personality, for words are the natural means of expressing thoughts and establishing understanding between people.'
>
> Maria Montessori (1939)

HOW DOES IT WORK?

Teaching strategies that focus on comprehension improves understanding by breaking down aspects of understanding into discrete steps. These are developed initially as skills, which are then practised so that they become automatic. The reader has to orchestrate these skills to comprehend the text as they read. Various reading strategies are shown in the table opposite, along with explanations of how you might explain them to learners.

Reading strategies

Predict — Determine what you think will happen in the text. Use clues in the title, headings and what you already know about it.

Visualise — Create mental images of what is happening, the characters, the setting and events in the text.

Question — Stop and ask questions to see how your understanding is building up. Re-read sections if there were parts you didn't follow.

Connect — Think about what you already know about the text. Think of ways to relate the text to others like it, to what you know about the context or background or how it relates to yourself or other people you know.

Identify — Work out what you think the author is doing. How do the details link to each other? Are there particular themes you can spot? What is the point of the story or text?

Infer — Use clues in the text and what you know already to fill in any gaps. What conclusions can you draw? Can you confirm any of these ideas as you continue reading?

Evaluate — Think about the text as a whole and make up your mind about what you think. Can you use evidence from the text to back up your opinions?

 # Principles

Principle 1: Goldilocks

The choice of text is crucial. It needs to be challenging to make the strategy useful, but not too difficult (avoid unfamiliar vocabulary, for example). It also needs to be interesting enough to hold the pupil's attention.

Principle 2: Bananarama

Don't stick with the same approach all year (such as guided reading or reciprocal teaching). Introduce new strategies over the course of the year so you can match the text to the strategy needed to extend pupils' current capabilities.

Unexpected finding

Computer-based tutoring approaches can be successful in improving reading comprehension particularly when developing self-questioning skills. This is good for practising strategies.

Teaching tips

✔ Check the level of difficulty you need for comprehension to extend pupils' reading capabilities. Ensure the texts you use are varied and provide an effective challenge.

✔ Use a range of strategies and approaches over the course of each term to provide variety and challenge. These will each need to be taught explicitly and practised consistently. Don't get stuck in a rut.

✔ Make sure learners are not struggling with basic decoding skills or vocabulary. Comprehension requires both of these. Effective diagnosis of reading difficulties is vital to identify possible solutions, particularly for older struggling readers.

✔ Teach for transfer. Focus learners' attention on the strategy they can apply more widely.

Leadership tips

✔ There are many successful reading comprehension strategies. Ensure teachers have access to a range of support and continuing professional development to extend their repertoire.

✔ Agree a progression in strategy use across key stages so pupils (and teachers) develop a repertoire of strategies.

KEY READINGS

Academic

Higgins, S., Henderson, P., Martell, T., Sharples, J. and Waugh, D. (2017), 'Improving literacy In Key Stage 1: Guidance report'. London: EEF, https://educationendowmentfoundation.org.uk/tools/guidance-reports/literacy-ks-1

Higgins, S., Martell, T., Waugh, D., Henderson, P. and Sharples, J. (2017), 'Improving literacy In Key Stage 2: Guidance report'. London: EEF, https://educationendowmentfoundation.org.uk/tools/guidance-reports/literacy-ks-2

Practical

Oakhill, J., Cain, K. and Elbro, C. (2014), *Understanding and Teaching Reading Comprehension*. Abingdon: Routledge.

11 HOMEWORK

⬆ **Attainment gain**	+ 5 months (secondary) + 2 months (primary)	-1 0 +1 **+2** +3 +4 **+5** +6 +7 +8

Learning benefits
- Improved time management.
- Organisational and study skills.
- Improved motivation, self-confidence and self-discipline.

Unexpected finding
- Homework has low impact for primary school pupils.

Teaching tips
- Link homework to lessons.
- Set frequent but short tasks.
- Mix it up – alternate between hard and easy tasks.
- Sow the seeds of study skills.
- Give feedback to pupils.
- Never use homework to penalise pupils.

Leadership tips
- Ensure teachers set clear, explicit learning aims.
- Try to coordinate homework from different departments.
- Pause before asking parents or carers to be involved in homework.
- Evaluate homework policies.

Principles
- Goldilocks
- Bananarama
- The Matthew Effect

WHAT IS IT?

Homework is any task for pupils to undertake outside normal school hours. The most effective homework has clear aims, is short and focussed, and complements classroom work. It should reinforce activities covered previously or preview topics to come. Some teachers prefer to call homework 'home learning' or 'extended learning'. It can encompass homework clubs organised at school or flipped learning where pupils digest information to be discussed in class. These differences relate to the different possible aims of homework. Some might want learners to get better at something they can do, but where they need more practice, such as reading. Some might want pupils to prepare for something new that you will build on in class, such as pre-learning spellings they will need, or to use flipped learning approaches.

DOES IT WORK?

Homework, if managed and monitored well for secondary school students, can lead to five months' extra progress over one academic year. Most studies show schools that give more homework perform better – but can't rule out the possibility that their better results could be due to something else the schools are doing rather than the homework itself. Does homework lead to better results or are high-achieving pupils simply doing more homework?

Homework is a risky teaching strategy. There is no qualified teacher present, little control over who completes the set tasks and plenty of potential distractions. Cheating is likely to be commonplace. It's little wonder the impact on achievement is so patchy – some studies have found little or no learning gains (Canadian Council on Learning, 2009). It makes it all the more important that any homework assigned is designed and delivered well.

One study found homework graded or commented on by teachers had twice the impact of homework without any feedback. Homework is particularly effective in mathematics and science (Canadian Council on Learning, 2009). There is little evidence it improves the attainment of primary school students (Farrow et al., 1999).

Learning benefits

Proponents of homework claim several non-academic benefits, including good independent study habits, improved time management and organisational skills, improved motivation and self-confidence, as well as the fostering of a sense of personal responsibility and self-discipline. It may promote a greater appreciation of schooling among parents.

> **'Effort is more important than time.'**
>
> Canadian Council on Learning (2009)

Others argue there is a lack of research proving these advantages. Opponents warn that homework can inhibit independent learning because students become preoccupied with work assigned by someone else. If left unchecked, homework can promote bad learning habits – copying answers, rushing tasks or studying in front of the television. In excess, it can cause stress and lead to less balanced and healthy lives.

HOW DOES IT WORK?

If pupils spend more time learning then they will improve. This can be through approaches like 'flipped learning' where they study new content in advance of the lesson so work in class can focus on the most challenging aspects of a topic. Homework can help consolidate skills to improve fluency (such as in number facts or learning vocabulary in modern foreign languages).

Principles

Principle 1: Goldilocks

Be careful not to demand too much homework. All study has a point of diminishing academic return. Hours slumped over a desk will test even the longest of attention spans. Children can become bored, stressed and demotivated. They'll turn off learning if assignments are too hard or not engaging enough.

Excessive homework can also backfire in other ways – encroaching on the time spent on sport, exercise, hobbies or relaxation and family life. When goals are unclear it can also create tensions with parents.

The 'ten-minute rule' is a helpful rule of thumb long advocated in the United States. It recommends a daily maximum of ten minutes of homework for every successive year group. Pupils in their first year of primary school at age five (Year 1), for example, should do no more than ten minutes of homework each night. Sixth formers (Year 12) should do no more than two hours, or 120 minutes. This advice has held firm over many decades.

> **'A good way to think about homework is the way you think about medications or dietary supplements. If you take too little, they'll have no effect. If you take too much, they can kill you. If you take the right amount, you'll get better.'**
>
> **Harris Cooper**

The research suggests a ceiling on beneficial home study of around two hours for older pupils (Cooper et al., 2006). Try to coordinate the homework set by different departments. Some homework is better than none, but too much can cause harm.

Principle 2: Bananarama

Quality of homework is more important than quantity. Set activities that embrace clear goals to engage students and encourage effort. The amount of effort, measured by how many of the tasks or questions are attempted, is a stronger prediction of future academic grades than the amount of time spent on homework.

Aim to enhance metacognitive or helicopter awareness of learning – having an oversight of how learning works. Students can improve their thinking about the way they learn – planning, doing and reviewing their work.

Principle 3: The Matthew Effect

Homework can exacerbate the achievement gap between poorer pupils and their more privileged peers. Disadvantaged children may get less help from their parents with their homework and have nowhere at home to study.

Studies have found the gap in test scores is larger in classes where homework was given compared with classes without homework. Yet other studies have shown homework, delivered well, can produce greater gains for lower-achieving pupils and benefit students from low-performing schools more than those at high-performing schools (Cooper et al., 2006). It all depends on the quality of the homework.

Unexpected finding

The evidence suggests homework has little impact on the attainment of primary school children (EEF, 2018d). Pupils are often set distinct projects during their primary school years rather than rehearsing specific topics already covered in the classroom. Parents end up doing more of the activities than they would care to admit. In secondary school, older students have developed as independent learners and are more able to block out external distractions.

Teaching tips

✓ Link homework to lessons. Home learning will work better if it dovetails with classroom learning: consolidating material covered in past lessons and offering a taster of what is to come. It should be an integral step on the learning journey, not a detour or distraction.

✓ Set frequent, short homework tasks rather than fewer lengthy assignments. This will sustain pupils' interest and attention when competing with the many distractions in a busy home. It's also good for learners to establish a regular routine.

✓ Mix it up. Pupils get turned off predictable work or disheartened if the tasks are too challenging. Alternate between hard and easy tasks. Get them to practise, revise or preview. Give pupils options to do more.

✓ Sow the seeds of study skills. Homework is an opportunity to nurture study skills – managing time, organising material and weighing up different learning strategies. These skills can be learned as well. Good study habits may be one of homework's most powerful lasting benefits.

✓ Give pupils focussed feedback on their completed homework. Feedback needs to be specific and timely and point to next steps in learning. Homework can help diagnose difficulties. But there's no need to grade or comment on every task.

✓ Nourish not punish. Never use homework to penalise pupils for poor performance or behaviour in class. Actions speak louder than words – children will come to see homework as punishment not nourishment.

Leadership tips

✓ Ensure your teachers are setting clear aims for homework. Teachers need to be clear to pupils and parents what specific goals they have in mind. There are many possible aims: reviewing material in class and finding whether pupils have understood a topic; previewing and preparing for topics to be covered at school; developing students' study skills; developing students into independent learners.

✓ Try to coordinate homework from different departments so students aren't burdened with work. Overloading them with homework will have diminishing impact.

✓ Pause before asking parents or carers to be involved in homework. They may have little time or expertise for helping out, or can't help rushing their children into completing tasks as quickly as possible. Learning can be lost in the uncontrollable environment of the home. However, it can be beneficial to share with parents the specific aims of homework, creating a bridge between schools and families. Consider a web-based texting system to get information home.

✓ Homework policies should be evaluated. Often homework is set for homework's sake, meeting the expectations of parents but having no benefit and taking up valuable teacher time. A policy should have clear rationale, responsibilities and review (see Anzac Park Public School's homework policy in the key readings for a good example).

KEY READINGS

Academic

Canadian Council on Learning (2009), 'A systematic review of literature examining the impact of homework on academic achievement', http://edu.au.dk/fileadmin/edu/Udgivelser/SystematicReview_HomeworkApril27-2009.pdf

Cooper, H., Robinson, J. C. and Patall, E. A. (2006), 'Does homework improve academic achievement? A synthesis of research, 1987–2003', *Review of Educational Research*, 76, (1), 1–62.

Practical

Anzac Park Public School, 'Homework policy', https://anzacpark-p.schools.nsw.gov.au/content/dam/doe/sws/schools/a/anzacpark-p/home-learning-/APPS_-_Home_Learning_Policy.pdf

Cooper, H. (2007), *The Battle Over Homework: Common ground for administrators, teachers, and parents* (3rd edn.). Thousand Oaks, CA: Corwin Press.

EEF (2018), 'Homework (primary)', *Sutton Trust-EEF Teaching and Learning Toolkit,* https://educationendowmentfoundation.org.uk/evidence-summaries/teaching-learning-toolkit/homework-primary/

EEF (2018), 'Homework (secondary)', *Sutton Trust-EEF Teaching and Learning Toolkit,* https://educationendowmentfoundation.org.uk/evidence-summaries/teaching-learning-toolkit/homework-secondary/

12 LEARNING STYLES

Attainment gain	+ 2 months	
Learning benefits	• Learning styles have more disadvantages than advantages. • They can limit learners' perceptions of themselves. • They can encourage teachers to blame a pupil's approach for their learning difficulties.	
Unexpected finding	• The psychological evidence does not support their existence!	
Teaching tips	• Don't use learning styles approaches. • Challenge learners to think of the best way to tackle a task. • Plan different ways to explain complex ideas. • Offer alternative ways of achieving learning objectives. • Focus on ensuring variety in teaching and on developing metacognition and self-regulation instead.	
Leadership tips	• Ban them in your school!	
Principles	• Bananarama • Goldilocks	

WHAT IS IT?

It is intuitively appealing that we each have a preferred approach or favourite way of doing something and that this works best for each of us. Researchers have found a host of different ways of describing these approaches and even more ways of assessing learners' individual preferences (Willingham et al., 2015).

The idea behind learning styles approaches is that as individuals we all have a particular approach or 'style of learning'. The theory is that learning will be more effective or more efficient if pupils are taught using the specific style or approach that has been identified as their personal learning style. For example, pupils categorised as having a 'listening' learning style could be taught more through storytelling and discussion and less through traditional written exercises. The problem with this enticing idea is that it is wrong (Pashler et al., 2008).

DOES IT WORK?

There is no robust evidence for any consistent set of learning 'styles' that can be used to identify genuine differences in the learning needs of young people. It is unhelpful to assign learners to groups or categories on the basis of a supposed learning style. The experimental evidence of the benefits of learning styles approaches is unconvincing due to problems with the designs of studies, the way learning styles are assessed and the outcomes used to measure impact (Aslaksen and Lorås, 2018).

> **'Measures of learning styles are invalid and students do not in fact learn better via their preferred modality.'**
>
> **BPS Research Digest (2018)**

The lack of impact of teaching to a particular learning style has been documented at all stages of education. The evidence shows an average impact of two months' progress for learning style interventions. However, given the limited evidence for the existence of learning styles, it is likely any gains are the result of pupils taking responsibility for their own learning (see self-regulation and metacognition, page 35) or from teachers using a wider range of activities to teach the same content.

Learning preferences do change in different situations and over time, and there is some evidence cognitive preference and task type may be connected (for example, visualisation is valuable for some areas of mathematics; see Carden and Cline, 2015). However, studies where teaching activities are targeted towards particular learners based on an identified learning 'style' have not shown any clear benefit, particularly for low-attaining pupils. It is especially important not to label primary-age pupils or for them to believe any lack of success is due to their learning style.

Learning benefits

Learning styles have no benefits that can't be achieved in other ways. In fact, learning styles have more disadvantages than advantages, as they can limit learners' perceptions of themselves and their abilities. They can also encourage teachers to blame learning difficulties on a pupil's approach to their learning.

HOW DOES IT WORK?

It doesn't! Any improvement is likely to be due to other factors, for example teachers consulting pupils about how they might best succeed or sharing responsibility with learners for how they tackle tasks. Learners may believe they can succeed too (see mastery learning,

> **'Matching instruction to learning styles has failed empirically.'**
>
> **Klein (2003)**

page 51) and this may change their behaviours, making them more persistent or resilient (see also self-regulation and metacognition, page 35).

 # Principles

Principle 1: Bananarama

There is no good way to do learning styles. Whilst some teachers have used learning styles approaches and have been successful, it's likely they were good teachers who mitigated all of the negative effects.

Principle 2: Goldilocks

Or rather, not Goldilocks, more the Big Bad Wolf! Learning styles aimed to develop learners' understanding of their own capability but missed the mark. It is more productive to focus on metacognition and self-regulation in developing learners' responsibility for their own learning.

Unexpected finding

Learning styles is not a robust or reliable idea to use in education. The surveys and questionnaires are unreliable. If you take them twice you are likely to get a different 'style'. Learners' preferences don't match with what they do. If you watch what learners do while learning, their approaches and choices do not correspond to what they say they prefer.

Teaching tips

✓ Don't encourage learners to think they have a preferred learning style. Instead, challenge them to think of the best way to tackle a task.

✓ Don't use a learning styles test or inventory. Instead, get learners to give examples of how and where they have improved.

✓ Do plan different ways to explain complex ideas and use images, diagrams, text, talk and sounds.

✓ Do offer alternative ways of achieving learning objectives. Make sure these support the way they will be assessed.

✓ Focus on metacognition and self-regulation and encourage learners to take responsibility for their own learning by recognising their strengths and areas to improve.

Leadership tips

✓ Ban learning styles approaches in your school! They are unscientific and can be limiting.

✓ Focus instead on metacognition and self-regulation, where learners take increasing responsibility for their own learning and motivation.

KEY READINGS

Academic

Aslaksen, K. and Lorås, H. (2018), 'The modality-specific learning style hypothesis: A mini-review', *Frontiers in Psychology*, 9, 1538.

BPS Research Digest (2018), 'An extra reason to abandon learning styles – teachers and pupils do not agree on the pupils' preferred learning style', https://digest.bps.org.uk/2018/12/12/an-additional-reason-to-abandon-learning-styles-teachers-and-pupils-do-not-agree-on-the-pupils-preferred-learning-style/

Pashler, H., McDaniel, M., Rohrer, D. and Bjork, R. (2008), 'Learning styles: Concepts and evidence', *Psychological Science in the Public Interest*, 9, (3), 105–119.

ACADEMIC SETTING

EDUCATION'S ZERO-SUM GAME

Attainment gain	– 1 month (between class) + 3 months (within class)	

 Learning benefits
- Can boost (but also harm) self-confidence, self-efficacy and growth mindset.
- Can lead to social segregation and damage educational equity.

 Unexpected finding
- It's better to be a big fish in a little pond and to do well in whatever group you find yourself.

Teaching tips
- Ensure an appropriate pace of learning in all sets.
- When grouping within a class, ensure pupils are organised separately for different subjects.
- Watch out for students struggling in higher sets.
- Focus on personal improvement over time and avoid competitive climates.
- Remember pupils in the same set are not the same.

 Leadership tips
- Consider carefully when to use the approach.
- Assign the best teachers to the lowest sets.
- Monitor whether children are moving in and out of sets and regroup different pupils for different subjects.

 Principles
- Bananarama
- The Matthew Effect

WHAT IS IT?

Academic setting refers to the grouping of children using their prior test results. Pupils with similar levels of attainment are grouped together either for specific lessons on a regular basis (known as setting or regrouping) or as a whole class (known as streaming or tracking). At earlier ages children are organised into different groups within the same class. Though often called 'ability' grouping, there are too many boys and summer-born children assigned to lower-ability sets or groups for this to be an accurate description.

DOES IT WORK?

Grouping children into different sets by 'ability' typically leads to no overall academic gains. Higher achievers enjoy a learning gain of one month or so over an academic year, but lower achievers lose the equivalent of one month's progress. The gains seen for higher achievers flourishing in the top sets is offset by the damage done to pupils languishing in the bottom classes.

However, flexible within-class grouping can be beneficial for all learners, providing an average benefit of three months' extra progress. Lower-attaining pupils benefit less than others, however, so this may still increase gaps in schools.

	Overall	High attainers	Low attainers
Between class	– 1 month	0 months	– 1 month
Within class	+ 3 months	+ 4 months	+ 2 months

 ## Learning benefits (and risks)

Recognising pupils as high achievers and giving them stretching tasks can enhance their confidence and aspirations. It can also be demoralising for pupils to be struggling when they are constantly behind the pace of their classroom peers. But it's easy to slip into a fixed mindset mentality. Rigid ability grouping can crush the self-belief of pupils who feel no amount of hard work will allow them to escape from the bottom of the class. We call them 'ability' groups, but they reflect *capability*, rather than a young person's potential or educational trajectory. Students are acutely aware of any ceilings imposed on their learning.

Confidence, self-efficacy and growth mindset

Social psychologist Albert Bandura (1982) defined self-efficacy as someone's belief in their ability to succeed in specific situations or accomplish a task. Your sense of self-efficacy can play a major role in how you approach goals, tasks and challenges. According to Bandura, self-efficacy differs from the colloquial term 'confidence'. Confidence is a general idea that refers to strength of belief but does not necessarily specify what the belief is about. Self-efficacy refers to a belief in your capabilities, that you can produce given levels of performance. A self-efficacy belief is both an idea of personal capability level and confidence in that capability.

Growth mindset, an idea coined by Stanford psychologist Carol Dweck (2017), is based on how learners react to failure. Dweck argues that individuals can be placed on a continuum depending on their implicit ideas about where ability comes from. Those with a 'fixed mindset' believe that abilities are mostly innate and interpret failure as the lack of necessary basic abilities, while those with a 'growth mindset' believe that they can acquire any given ability provided they invest effort or study. Growth mindset can be seen as the way that learners interpret their own agency and self-efficacy in response to failure.

HOW DOES IT WORK?

The assumption is that it will be possible to teach more effectively or more efficiently with a narrower range of attainment in a class. Based on the evidence, this is a risky assumption as the average impact is negative when children are organised into different classes. One study suggested no positive impact on maths or English outcomes from setting despite attempts to improve how children were taught once they were grouped by 'ability' (Roy et al., 2018).

Grouping younger children onto separate tables in the same class enables teachers to differentiate activities for children. Teaching can then be catered to the individual learning needs of different groups of pupils. This may mean providing more demanding tasks for children who have already mastered a topic, or offering more support for others who are struggling. (It doesn't mean adapting to different 'learning styles' – see page 73.)

 ## Principles

Principle 1: Bananarama

Studies reveal little of how children are taught once they have been assigned to different classrooms or schools (Gamoran, 1992). Any difference in pupil outcomes is due to teachers changing the way they teach and what they teach to the classes. It's not what practice is adopted but how it's delivered that matters. It's about the quality of instruction for the specific learning needs of individual pupils.

> 'What matters most comes next: decisions about what to do with students after they've been assigned to classes. Given poor instruction, neither heterogeneous nor homogeneous grouping can be effective; with excellent instruction, either may succeed.'
>
> Adam Gamoran (1992)

Principle 2: The Matthew Effect

In theory, sets could be a vehicle for social mobility for disadvantaged pupils enabling them to fulfil their academic potential. The problem in practice is they don't benefit from the support and private tutoring outside school enjoyed by their more privileged peers (Kirby, 2016). Disadvantaged students are more likely to fall into lower sets – even when they have demonstrated academic potential. They may suffer the full force of the Matthew Effect: 'even what they have shall be taken away'. You must try to assess academic potential as well as achievement. A general rule is the more rigid the setting is, the bigger the inequality between higher and lower achievers.

Unexpected finding

It's better to be a big fish in a little pond. High achievers in top sets can suffer a blow to their confidence. This is due to a universal human tendency: we judge ourselves against those closest to us. Children used to coming first in class – the big fishes in a little pond – experience a sinking feeling when they realise they are near the bottom of a class of higher-achieving peers.

Students ranked lowly in top academic sets or selective schools suffer from lower academic confidence – or 'academic self-concept' – than equally high-achieving students in lower sets or non-selective schools. The higher the average attainment of the class, the bigger the blow to self-belief. More anxious students experience larger effects. The 'big fish little pond effect' punctures the assumption that all children benefit from being selected to a top academic set, stream or school. It is replicated for students across all ages and capabilities, from primary schools to universities (Gamoran, 1992). As Malcolm Gladwell (2014) says, 'Rarely do we stop and consider whether the most prestigious of institutions is always in our best interest. The Big Pond takes really bright students and demoralizes them.'

Teaching tips

✓ Consider the pace of learning in lower sets and how students can catch up on parts of the curriculum they miss. Problem solving, critical thinking and higher-order metacognitive prompts occur more frequently in top sets. Teachers in low sets spend more time on managing behaviour.

✓ When grouping within a class, ensure pupils are organised separately for different subjects. Think about which activities are grouped by levels of attainment and which are not.

✓ Watch out for students struggling in higher sets – the small fishes in big ponds. Counter students' inclination to compare their academic accomplishments with their peers.

✓ Focus feedback and assessment on forming pupils' self-evaluations of personal improvement over time, emphasising prior achievement, effort and learning. Competitive climates should be avoided if they promote negative comparisons. These principles apply equally to pupils in mixed-ability classes.

✓ Remember that together is not the same. Academic setting can create an exaggerated sense of within-group homogeneity and between-group heterogeneity.

✓ Be careful not to underestimate the range of different levels of understanding and individual feedback needs within the same 'ability' group.

✓ Watch out for over-compensating between groups, going too fast with the high-ability groups and too slow with the lowest sets.

Leadership tips

✓ Assign the most effective teachers to the lowest sets. They are the ones who need the most support in school. Children who enjoy less support outside school are likely to have the largest potential learning gains inside school.

✓ Adopt a flexible approach to setting, allowing children to move in and out of sets and grouping different pupils for different subjects.

✓ Constantly reassess students' capabilities. Look for indications of what they may be capable of in the future. You can often tell from how quickly learners respond to help. If they only require a small nudge then this is often an indication of greater capability.

✓ Avoid permanent arrangements that create a downward spiral of low expectations among teachers and pupils.

KEY READINGS

Academic

Fang, J., Huang, X., Zhang, M., Huang, F., Li, Z. and Yuan, Q. (2018), 'The big-fish-little-pond effect on academic self-concept: A meta-analysis', *Frontiers in Psychology*, 9, 1569, www.ncbi.nlm.nih.gov/pmc/articles/PMC6124391

Gamoran, A. (1992), 'Synthesis of research: Is ability grouping equitable?', *Educational Leadership*, 50, 11–17, www.ascd.org/publications/educational-leadership/oct92/vol50/num02/Synthesis-of-Research-~-Is-Ability-Grouping-Equitable%C2%A2.aspx

Gutiérrez, R. and Slavin, R. E. (1992), 'Achievement effects of the nongraded elementary school: A best evidence synthesis', *Review of Educational Research*, 62, (4), 333–376.

Marsh, H. W., Seaton, M., Trautwein, U., Lüdtke, O., Hau, K. T., O'Mara, A. J. and Craven, R. G. (2008), 'The big-fish–little-pond-effect stands up to critical scrutiny: Implications for theory, methodology, and future research', *Educational Psychology Review*, 20, (3), 319–350, https://link.springer.com/article/10.1007/s10648-008-9075-6

Puzio, K. and Colby, G. (2010), 'The effects of within class grouping on reading achievement: a meta-analytic synthesis', Society for Research on Educational Effectiveness, https://eric.ed.gov/?id=ED514135

Roy, P., Styles, B., Walker, M., Morrison, J., Nelson, J. and Kettlewell, K. (2018), 'Best practice in grouping students intervention A: Best practice in setting'. London: EEF. https://educationendowmentfoundation.org.uk/public/files/Projects/Evaluation_Reports/Intervention_A_-_Best_Practice_in_Setting.pdf

14 DIGITAL TECHNOLOGIES

MORE THAN MOTIVATING THE RELUCTANT LEARNER

 Attainment gain +4 months

 Learning benefits
- Young people may be more engaged – but in learning or technology?

 Unexpected finding
- Technology works better when it supplements rather than replaces teaching.

 Teaching tips
- Identify your teaching and learning goal first.
- Consider how digital technology will boost learning.
- Remember pupils' motivation to use technology does not always translate into more effective learning.

 Leadership tips
- Be clear about what any new technology will replace.
- Assess costs.
- Allocate time for teachers to learn how to teach well with any new digital tool.
- Choose tried-and-tested technologies.

 Principles
- Bananarama
- Goldilocks

WHAT IS IT?

There is now a vast range of digital technologies that can be used to support teaching and learning in schools. There are all kinds of digital devices and tools, from mobile phones to interactive displays, from calculators to Khan Academy. Approaches in this area vary enormously, but involve either of the following:

- technology for students, where learners use programmes or applications designed for problem solving or open-ended learning
- technology for teachers, such as interactive whiteboards or learning platforms.

> '**Books will soon be obsolete in the public schools. Scholars will be instructed through the eye. It is possible to teach every branch of human knowledge with the motion picture. Our school system will be completely changed inside of ten years.**'
>
> **Thomas Edison (1913)**

DOES IT WORK?

Digital technology can be used to bring about modest improvements in attainment, producing on average an extra four months' progress over a year, but there is considerable variation in impact when comparing different resources, tools and how they are used.

It is unlikely that particular technologies bring about changes in learning directly, but some have the potential to enable changes in teaching and learning habits. For example, they can support teachers to provide more effective feedback or use more helpful representations, or they can motivate students to practise more. Focus on the learning, not the technology!

> '**Computers meet classroom; classroom wins**'
>
> **Larry Cuban (1993)**

Learning benefits

Research often reports children and young people are more engaged when using technology. The question is: are they more engaged in learning or just in using technology? We need to be careful to distinguish between being engaged in the task, the technology or working with others and actually being engaged in the learning (Higgins et al., 2012). Are the pupils just having fun, or are there indications of engagement in learning from what they are talking about or the questions they ask?

HOW DOES IT WORK?

Technology can help you zoom in on a skill, such as copy and paste and inserting text when redrafting. This is much more efficient than rewriting. It can also motivate learners to try again until they succeed, such as when using an online learning tutorial like Khan Academy. Alternatively, they can help with recording, such as taking a photograph as a record to look back on. The wide range of possibilities makes it hard to be prescriptive, but it's about how well you use technology rather than whether you use any particular tool or digital device. We suspect most of the time it works because pupils just learn for longer with digital technologies.

 # Principles

Principle 1: Bananarama

It's not about having tablets or touch-screen tables; it's about integrating these technologies for teaching and learning. Technology can help focus on specific skills and strategies aligned to your learning objectives. Using a word processor makes moving text around, inserting and deleting easy (at least compared with on paper) so it's great for redrafting. It is not so good for text entry (unless you've taught touch typing). Teaching redrafting on pre-prepared texts avoids this challenge.

Principle 2: Goldilocks

Be careful the technology does not mask the learning. If pupils use a spell check, you can't assess their spelling. Identify what you can assess and where the technology may have supported them. Practising number facts on a computer may well be motivating, but make sure you still give timed tests to check for progress.

Unexpected finding

Digital technologies work better when they supplement rather than replace teaching. Technology is better at consolidating learning than introducing new ideas. It may be learners like using it so it motivates practice and helps them to see the connections between what they do in the digital world and what they do in the real world.

Teaching tips

✓ Identify your teaching and learning goal first, then consider how digital technology could help.

✓ Pupils won't learn more unless they spend more time learning, or learn more efficiently or more effectively, with digital technology. Which do you think it will be and how will you know?

✓ Remember that pupils' motivation to use technology does not always translate into more effective learning, particularly if the use of the technology and the desired learning outcomes aren't aligned.

Leadership tips

✓ Be clear about what any new technology will replace. What will teachers stop doing? How do you know the digital approach will be better for pupils' learning?

✓ Have you thought through the lifetime costs of any new digital technology? When will it need replacing and how will you afford it?

✓ Have you allocated enough time for teachers to learn how to teach well with any new digital tool? This takes longer than you think and means that staff can use it fluently, not just know how to turn it on!

✓ Choose tried-and-tested technologies, unless you are prepared to invest in a technician too.

KEY READINGS

Academic

Morphy, P. and Graham, S. (2012), 'Word processing programs and weaker writers/readers: A meta-analysis of research findings', *Reading and Writing*, 25, (3), 641–678.

Practical

EEF (2018), 'Digital technology', *Sutton Trust-EEF Teaching and Learning Toolkit,* https://educationendowmentfoundation.org.uk/resources/teaching-learning-toolkit/digital-technology

The EEF also published a review of the use of digital technologies for learning: https://educationendowmentfoundation.org.uk/public/files/Publications/The_Impact_of_Digital_Technologies_on_Learning_(2012).pdf. Have a look at the six myths in Appendix 1.

McNally, S., Ruiz-Valenzuela, J. and Rolfe, H. (2016), 'ABRA: Online reading support evaluation report and executive summary, October 2016'. London: EEF.

15 SMALLER CLASSES

	Attainment gain	+ 3 months 
	Learning benefits	• Less stress for teachers. • Improved behaviour.
	Unexpected finding	• It is not cost effective to make classes smaller to improve attainment.
	Teaching tips	• Consider what approach is best for learners at a particular point in their development. • Deploy other staff to best effect. • In a larger class use strategies that get more feedback to individual pupils.
	Leadership tips	• Consider smaller classes for younger pupils. • Think about how extra staff are deployed during whole-class teaching. • Do not increase class sizes!
	Principles	• Bananarama • Threshold Effect

WHAT IS IT?

Class sizes vary, but most schools in developed countries have 20 to 30 pupils in a class. Having fewer pupils in a class is often seen as desirable, but is it effective? It feels easier to teach smaller classes, but the evidence suggests the benefits in terms of learning are outweighed by the additional costs of extra teachers and classrooms.

DOES IT WORK?

It may seem obvious that reducing the number of pupils in a class will improve the quality of classroom teaching, but it in fact has only a small impact on pupil progress. This is disappointing given the high costs of employing more teachers.

There is evidence that younger children and children from disadvantaged backgrounds may benefit more directly from being taught in smaller classes (Vaag Iversen and Bonesrønning, 2013).

 ## Learning benefits

Although the impact on attainment is low, there are other reported benefits to reducing the number of pupils in a class. Teachers are less stressed and smaller classes suffer from fewer behaviour problems. These are important factors to consider, but in terms of attainment, you'd be better off investing in extra teachers or teaching assistants for one-to-one or intensive small-group teaching (see teaching assistants, page 25, and one-to-one tuition, page 29).

HOW DOES IT WORK?

The theory is that a smaller class or teaching group increases the range of approaches a teacher can employ and the amount of attention each pupil receives, improving outcomes for pupils. However, it is hard for teachers to change what they do unless the class is very small (up to 17 pupils; Nye et al., 2002), so this doubles the cost of teaching. It is also possible that pupils get more feedback in smaller classes, though we should be cautious about this as too much individualisation can be detrimental (see page 21). Smaller classes also have less disruption, so it may not all be about what the teacher does (McKee et al., 2015).

 ## Principles

Principle 1: Bananarama

It's not having smaller classes; it's how well you teach in the class you have. There are things you can do differently in smaller classes. Teachers can make more observations of pupils' progress and will have time to address difficulties as they arise.

Principle 2: Threshold Effect

The benefits of smaller classes don't kick in until they have well under 20 pupils. This is probably because of the flexibility a smaller class gives you. It is easier to monitor two other groups of six pupils while you focus on four pupils rather than four other groups. You can also work through the groups in a couple of days rather than a week.

Unexpected finding

It is not cost effective to make classes smaller to improve attainment. There is a link between class size and learning, and pupils in smaller classes do tend to do better. However, unless you can afford to reduce classes to 15 pupils, the investment is not worthwhile.

Teaching tips

✓ Think about what teaching approaches are best for learners at a particular point in their development – whether it is whole-class teaching, small-group work or targeted one-to-one tuition.

✓ How can you deploy other staff to best effect (see teaching assistants, page 25)?

✓ In a larger class, think about how you can get more feedback to individuals. Consider techniques such as peer-assessment, icons or stickers, or group feedback.

Leadership tips

✓ Consider smaller classes for younger pupils to get them off to a flying start. It may be worth the investment here.

✓ How are extra staff deployed during whole-class teaching? Are they sitting watching or working one-to-one or with a small group?

✓ Small reductions in class size are not worthwhile so don't spend money on them unless you can afford to reduce classes to 15 pupils or fewer.

✓ Smaller classes may not be cost effective, but this does not justify increasing class sizes!

KEY READINGS

Academic

Blatchford, P., Chan, K. W., Maurice, G., Lai, K. C. and Lee, J. C. K. (eds.) (2016), *Class Size: Eastern and western perspectives*. Abingdon: Routledge.

Department for Education (2011), 'Class size and education in England evidence report', www.gov.uk/government/uploads/system/uploads/attachment_data/file/183364/DFE-RR169.pdf

EEF (2018), 'Reducing class sizes', *Sutton Trust-EEF Teaching and Learning Toolkit*, https://educationendowmentfoundation.org.uk/resources/teaching-learning-toolkit/reducing-class-size/

SUMMER-BORN DISADVANTAGE

 Attainment gain — 3 months

 Learning benefits

Addressing summer-born disadvantage:
- Preserves self-confidence and self-esteem.
- Avoids higher risks of underage smoking.
- Prevents misdiagnosis of learning difficulties.

 Unexpected finding
- Autumn-born pupils are more likely to become professional sportspeople.

 Teaching tips
- Monitor the progress of summer-born pupils as you would do for other vulnerable groups.
- Address low expectations and lack of confidence.
- Consider age when appointing pupils into leadership roles at school.
- Talk about the maturity of pupils when discussing their progress with parents.
- Adjust any academic or sporting selection to take into account the different ages and physical development of children.

 Leadership tips
- Assess students in an age-adjusted way.
- Do not allow parents to delay school entry for their children.

Principles
- Goldilocks
- The Matthew Effect

WHAT IS IT?

Children born between June and August do less well at school on average than their autumn-born classmates (Crawford et al., 2013). Summer-born pupils are more likely to have special educational needs, to have lower self-esteem, to be less confident in their own abilities, and to be more prone to falling into risky behaviour (Sykes et al., 2009). When you are born matters.

The birthdate effect has been revealed across the world – students born during the initial months of the school year enjoy a lasting academic advantage compared with those born in later months. The pattern is also observed in sport, with those born just after a cut-off date more likely to be selected for teams (Helsen et al., 2013). Some refer to it as the relative age effect (RAE) but a more accurate description might be the 'Age at Test Effect': younger pupils do less well as they are less mature when they are assessed in tests and exams.

A simple way of tackling much of this inequity would be to calculate age-adjusted scores in examinations and tests, assessing a child's progress relative to others at their age, rather than older pupils in their class. Expected levels of progress would apply to a particular age rather than a particular point in time. Schools would be judged in league tables on these fairer tests. It's also important to consider maturity when grouping children into sets or classes according to their achievement. The difference it makes is important. Summer-born pupils are on average six months behind their older peers at age seven, three months behind at age 12, and still a month behind at age 16. In England, summer-born teenagers were 6.4 percentage points less likely to achieve the national benchmark of five GCSEs or equivalents at grades A* to C. Here we have converted the effect size from correlational studies to make it equivalent to studies found in the *Sutton Trust-EEF Teaching and Learning Toolkit*. As we noted in the introduction the effect is not like the approaches in the toolkit where there is stronger evidence of benefit. Here we are looking at the extent of the gap these approaches would need to close.

Delaying school entry for some pupils won't solve the birthdate effect as there will always be younger children in the classroom who are less mature.

> 'We need to replace the patchwork of lucky breaks and arbitrary advantages today that determine success – the fortunate birth dates and the happy accidents of history – with a society that provides opportunities for all.'
>
> Malcolm Gladwell (2009)

DOES IT WORK?

Recognising summer-born disadvantage could improve the progress of younger learners. One of the issues here is that we don't notice the impact on individuals. We all know summer-born children who have been successful. What we don't know is how much more successful they might have been had they been born a month or two later and had the advantage of being the oldest in the year. Summer-born children are spread throughout the range in the class, with some just a little behind their peers. It is only when you look at the big picture you can see the overall effect on this group.

These differences can be life defining if younger children miss out on the cut-off point for academic selection at school, entry into sixth form or university admissions. There are far more autumn-born pupils in the top streams when primary school pupils are grouped together by 'ability'. Older pupils are more likely to be selected for gifted and talented programmes. One study found September-born students are 20 per cent more likely to go to university than their August-born peers (Sykes et al., 2009).

Being summer born is a big disadvantage for poorer children without support at home. Success in school is influenced by date of birth across the entire curriculum in reading, writing, science and mathematics. Being just one month younger than a fellow pupil can lower attainment.

Learning benefits

There are many potential benefits of helping summer-born children – both in their social and emotional development and their academic progress. They are nearly twice as likely to suffer from behavioural difficulties and are at higher risk of underage smoking (Crawford et al., 2013). Many are misdiagnosed as having special educational needs by teachers who confuse immaturity with learning problems. They are more prone to low self-esteem and a lack of confidence in their own capability.

The good news is these disadvantages tend not to persist into adulthood. Researchers found the summer-born were as likely to be in work and earn as much as their older peers, and as likely to be as healthy and happy (Crawford et al., 2013). It is just in school that this disadvantage appears.

HOW DOES IT WORK?

You should treat summer-born children like any other vulnerable groups of pupils – monitoring their progress in relation to what is expected for their age, taking care not to discriminate against younger children when selecting pupils for classroom activities or school leadership opportunities. Age-adjusted tests scale up scores for younger pupils so they are compared with their own age group.

> 'These differences in educational attainment and other skills and behaviours may affect children's well-being in the short term... they may have potentially serious long-term consequences for children's lives.'
>
>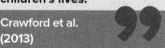
>
> Crawford et al. (2013)

Principles

Principle 1: Goldilocks

It is important to get testing and assessment 'just right'. The age at which a child sits a test is the main reason for the attainment gap between those born at the start of the school year and those born at the end. Autumn-born children are, on average, more cognitively, biologically and emotionally mature than their summer-born classmates. It's little surprise they perform better. It is not that they have lower 'ability'; it is just that they are younger. This is sometimes called the 'age-at-test' effect and is found consistently across school systems that start at different times of the year.

In the reception class at primary school, the eldest pupils have lived 25 per cent longer than the youngest pupils; by school-leaving age, they are six per cent older. The test score advantages they enjoy mirror these relative age differences – shrinking at the same rate as children age. Doing less well in tests can have a number of knock-on effects for summer-born pupils, undermining their self-confidence. It is these effects we should try to mitigate in schools.

Principle 2: The Matthew Effect

The 'age-at-test' effect however doesn't explain the entire summer disadvantage attainment gap. The Matthew Effect means that the initial advantage that older children have tends to be maintained. August-born pupils (or those youngest in their school year) suffer from lower self-esteem because of how they see themselves relative to other pupils in the pecking order of the class. If pupils think of themselves as low achievers compared with more mature pupils, this can become a self-fulfilling prophecy. It's their relative position that matters. This relative age effect also contributes to lower test scores, which again influences learners' judgements of themselves.

> **'In a less enlightened era, astrologists would have had a field day. Across the terrain of youth football in England, individuals born in September are doing far better than those born in August.'**
>
> **Matthew Syed (2011)**

Unexpected finding

Being bigger and better-coordinated, older children are more likely to be selected for sports teams. The impact of birthdate is prevalent in football, rugby and netball teams where there is competition for places (Cobley et al., 2008). Older students score higher on average in assessments of cardiovascular fitness, muscle strength and ability to accelerate. They run faster, jump higher and are more powerful than younger peers. They get more support and coaching, and are more likely to become elite players.

Surveys show older pupils in their year group are more likely to become professional sportspeople (Musch and Hay, 1999). The Football Association for example found 57 per cent of players at Premier League academies were born between September and December, compared with 14 per cent who had their birthday between May and August (Jackson, 2011). We miss out on talent by failing to distinguish between physical maturity and sporting ability.

Teaching tips

✓ Be vigilant of the disadvantages children born later in the academic year face, and share best practice in reducing achievement gaps.

✓ Monitor the progress and wellbeing of summer-borns as you would do for other vulnerable groups such as children with English as an additional language or those receiving free school meals. Particular attention should be paid to address low expectations and lack of confidence. Keep an eye out for summer-borns being referred for special needs or indulging in risky behaviour.

✓ Consider age when appointing pupils into leadership roles.

✓ Remember to consider the age and maturity of pupils when discussing their progress with parents. Be sympathetic to summer-born students who wish to re-sit their GCSE or A-level examinations.

✓ Adjust selection for sports teams to take into account the different ages and physical development of children. Selection should not be based on physical maturity.

Leadership tips

✓ Assess students in chronological age bands (by month of birth or season of birth) rather than as a whole class. Any test or assessment should be age adjusted so pupils are judged equally. This is particularly important when selecting for school, sixth form or college admissions or when grouping children into sets or classes according to their achievement.

✓ Allowing parents to delay entry for their children into school won't help address the birthdate effect. Children do better in tests because they are more developed, not because they have had more time in school.

KEY READINGS

Academic

Crawford, C., Dearden, L. and Greaves, E. (2013), 'When you are born matters: Evidence for England', *IFS Reports* (No. R80). London: Institute for Fiscal Studies.

Helsen, W. F., Baker, J., Schorer, J., Van Winckel, J. and Williams, M. A. (2013), 'The relative age effect in European Professional Soccer: Is there any difference after ten years of research?', *Journal of Exercise, Movement, and Sport*, 45, (1).

Sykes, E. D. A., Bell, J. F. and Rodeiro, C. V. (2009), 'Birthdate effects: A review of the literature from 1990-on'. Cambridge: Cambridge Assessment. www.cambridgeassessment.org.uk/Images/109784-birthdate-effects-a-review-of-the-literature-from-1990-on.pdf

17 PREPARING TO LEARN

Attainment gain	+ 2 months	

Learning benefits	• Healthier living and improved wellbeing. • Reduced risks of major illnesses. • Improved attendance and behaviour.
Unexpected finding	• Attending a pre-school breakfast club but not eating can improve attainment.
Teaching tips	• Factor in extra time needed for these programmes. • Consider what types of intervention are required for different age groups. • Develop clear instructions on how to implement programmes. • Promote the benefits of healthier lifestyles to parents. • Sensitively target pupils most likely to benefit.
Leadership tips	• Create a culture that embraces healthier living, wellbeing and readiness to learn. • Recognise the extra time and work school staff need to develop and implement programmes.
Principles	• The Matthew Effect • Multiplier Effect

WHAT IS IT?

There are a number of things we can do to help make sure that children and young people are prepared to learn in schools. In this chapter, we will look at several areas where there is evidence that this preparation can help pupils learn better. This does not come from the *Sutton Trust-EEF Teaching and Learning Toolkit*, but from other studies about wider aspects of health and wellbeing, such as providing meals or glasses for reading. These don't always have a direct impact on progress but are worth checking to see if they are hindering pupils in their learning.

Enabling children to live healthier lives – eating better, sleeping well and being fit in body and mind – are all essential for healthier learning.

Programmes range from offering free universal breakfasts and lunches for pupils, to advising children on how to get a decent night's sleep, encouraging them to exercise and ensuring they get glasses for poor eyesight. Other interventions aim to improve children's wellbeing, for example teaching mindfulness techniques, cognitive behavioural therapy, and raising awareness about anxiety, depression and other mental health issues.

DOES IT WORK?

Free universal breakfast before school or free meals at lunch time can boost attainment. A recent EEF study of breakfast clubs produced an average of two months' extra progress for primary school pupils during the academic year (EEF, 2018e).

Sleep education programmes show some promise in addressing teenagers' lack of sleep. Insufficient sleep among teenagers whose brains are programmed to sleep and wake later than adults has been recognised as an important public health issue, but we have yet to demonstrate that these interventions can improve sleep and school outcomes (Dewald et al., 2010).

> **'There is a time for many words, and there is also a time for sleep.'**
> Homer

Studies outside the UK have found that enabling children to wear glasses improves academic attainment by an extra two months in one academic year (see for example Ma et al., 2014). Around ten to 15 per cent of children fail their mandatory eyesight test in the UK, but a third of those children aren't taken to the opticians to obtain glasses.

Research suggests incorporating moderate to vigorous activity into lessons can improve academic progress (Public Health England, 2014). There is also good evidence that programmes aimed at promoting pupils' resilience and wellbeing can boost academic results. Children's non-cognitive skills – including motivation, perseverance and self-control – have been linked with improved school results and other positive outcomes in later life, for example financial stability and reduced crime. But so far the evidence is not convincing enough to conclude this is a causal relationship (Gutman and Schoon, 2013b).

Learning benefits

These programmes have the potential to make children's lives healthier and more productive. One result is improved attendance and behaviour at school, which can lead to better academic progress. But the potential gains in later life are much broader than this. Exercising regularly and healthy eating lower the risk of major illnesses and stress, and can boost

> **'If more of us valued food and cheer and song above hoarded gold, it would be a merrier world.'**
> J.R.R. Tolkien

self-esteem and sleep quality. Being more motivated, exhibiting more grit, and regulating emotions and behaviour in the face of temptations and impulses are all valuable assets as important for life as academic grades.

HOW DOES IT WORK?

Providing hungry and malnourished children with nutritious food low in sugar, salt and fat enables them to focus on learning. Addressing sleep deprivation or lack of exercise can improve concentration and behaviour in the classroom and boost attainment. The question is how much time and resource teachers have to deal with learning impediments that come from outside school.

In one sleep education programme, Teensleep, teachers deliver ten half-hour lessons highlighting the importance of sleep, and offer practical tips for improving sleep, such as avoiding caffeine and blue light in the evening. A pilot study published by the EEF (2019b) found no evidence of improved sleep, but students reported napping less often.

In Glasses for Classes, the results of eye tests are shared with vision coordinators, school staff trained to support pupils to get glasses and wear them (EEF, 2019c). Funding is provided for a second pair of glasses for pupils to keep at school.

Physically Active Lessons (PAL) adapt lesson plans to include short bursts of physical activity with academic content. The aim is to introduce ten to 15 minutes of exercise twice daily every day of the week (EEF, 2017c).

Cognitive behavioural therapy is used in programmes that aim to improve pupils' wellbeing, resilience and motivation. The programmes take one hour per week and replace schools' current personal, social, and health education lessons (EEF, 2019d).

 Principles

Principle 1: The Matthew Effect

Addressing the stark inequalities in health and wellbeing outside school has the potential to improve the attainment of disadvantaged pupils in the classroom. There is an extensive research literature demonstrating that acute gaps in healthy living between children from poorer backgrounds and their richer peers limit their chance to live longer, healthier lives. Disadvantaged children are less likely to get regular exercise and eat balanced diets, as well as experiencing other issues that can affect their learning directly such as receiving glasses after being diagnosed with poor eyesight in an eye test. These factors can exert a profound impact on children's ability to learn.

Principle 2: Multiplier Effect

Breakfast club schools experience a multiplier effect – seeing an improvement in the behaviour of pupils in general. This may be due to less disruption in class from hungry pupils or pupils arriving late. It makes for better classroom environments.

Unexpected finding

A trial of Magic Breakfast, a programme offering free universal breakfasts for primary school children, particularly in disadvantaged areas, found it wasn't eating breakfast that made the difference to pupils, but merely attending the breakfast club (EEF, 2018e). It may be that experiencing a session before the school day prepares pupils for learning by providing a routine before school starts.

Teaching tips

✓ Plan for the extra time you'll need to prepare for programmes that aren't about core classroom teaching.

✓ Develop a clear set of instructions on how to implement the programme so it can be run consistently and effectively.

✓ Consider what types of intervention are required for different age groups – sleep deprivation is a teenage issue; breakfasts are particularly beneficial for younger children.

✓ Promote activities to parents to encourage participation, communicating the benefits of healthier lifestyles.

✓ Encourage all children to attend while sensitively targeting the pupils who are most likely to benefit.

Leadership tips

✓ Do as you say: create a culture, ethos and environment that embrace healthier living, wellbeing and readiness to learn.

✓ Recognise the extra time and work school staff need to develop and implement programmes. What less effective activities can be reduced to free up time?

KEY READINGS

Academic

Blunden, S. and Rigney, G. (2015), 'Lessons learned from sleep education in schools: A review of dos and don'ts', *Journal of Clinical Sleep Medicine*, 11, (6), 671–680, www.ncbi.nlm.nih.gov/pmc/articles/PMC4442228/

Brown, V., Crawford, C., Dearden, L., Greaves, E., Kitchen, S., Payne, C., Purdon, S. and Tanner, E. (2012), 'Evaluation of the free school meals pilot: Impact report'. London: Department for Education. www.ifs.org.uk/publications/6279

Slavin, R. E., Collins, M. E., Repka, M. X., Friedman, D. S., Mudie, L. I., Owoeye, J. O. and Madden, N. A. (2018), 'In plain sight: Reading outcomes of providing eyeglasses to disadvantaged children', *Journal of Education for Students Placed at Risk*, 23, (3), 250–258.

Practical

Crawford, C., Edwards, A., Farquharson, C., Greaves, E., Trevelyan, G., Wallace, E. and White, C. (2016), 'Magic Breakfast: Evaluation report and executive summary'. London: EEF. https://educationendowmentfoundation.org.uk/public/files/Projects/Evaluation_Reports/Magic_Breakfast.pdf

Public Health England (2014), 'The link between pupil health and wellbeing and attainment: A briefing for head teachers, governors and staff in education settings', https://assets.publishing.service.gov.uk/government/uploads/system/uploads/attachment_data/file/370686/HT_briefing_layoutvFINALvii.pdf

18 INDIVIDUALISED LEARNING

 Attainment gain +3 months

 Learning benefits
- Develops independence and personal responsibility.

 Unexpected finding
- It is harder than it looks to do well!

 Teaching tips
- Make sure it is a good use of your pupils' time.
- Count the cost of preparing, managing and monitoring multiple tasks.
- Use it in short bursts to keep pupils motivated.
- Use it to complement other approaches.

 Leadership tips
- Make sure it's a good use of teachers' time.
- Identify good digital technology solutions that are as self-managing as possible.

 Principles
- Goldilocks
- The Matthew Effect

WHAT IS IT?

Individualised learning is where pupils are given different tasks and provided with individual support and feedback. It is based on the idea that all learners have different needs and may learn at a different pace from each other. An approach that is personally tailored should be more effective (EEF, 2018f).

Various models of individualised learning have been tried, particularly in subjects like mathematics (Horak, 1981), where pupils can have individual sets of activities to complete. The teacher takes a monitoring role in managing the tasks and in supporting the learner. Digital technologies have been used to provide more individualised activities and feedback through tutorial programmes (Steenbergen-Hu and Cooper, 2013). It is sometimes also called personalised learning, though some argue that for learning to be fully personalised, learners should have some choice about what they learn.

Individualised or personalised learning can support other approaches such as a mastery approach (see page 51), where it is used to ensure learners keep up with class progress. It can be a way of applying metacognitive skills or developing greater self-regulation (see page 35) by teaching strategies or techniques that learners apply independently. It is different from an approach such as one-to-one tuition (see page 29) in that the focus is on activities that are independent of the teacher. The teacher tends to adopt a less direct approach and monitors progress.

Of course, there are some children who need a specific plan or programme of support that is individualised. We are not talking about this here, important though it is. This chapter is about systematic approaches that aim to individualise or tailor lessons for all pupils.

DOES IT WORK?

Individualised learning works when learners are motivated and capable (see metacognition and self-regulated learning, page 35) and can develop independence and greater confidence in learning. The tasks and activities need to be at the right level of challenge for the learner to succeed in making progress (not so easy they aren't learning anything and not so hard they can't manage on their own). It may not work well until learners have the capability to work on their own (Connor et al., 2013). It can also be time consuming to prepare and manage. Research shows that it works better for older pupils, and in shorter blocks (Boden et al., 2000).

'The reality… is that many schools purchase off-the-shelf software and call it "personalized learning," without being able to say what is supposed to change in the classroom. And even when schools do take a broader view, they often fail to recognize that success depends largely on decisions that educators and administrators make on the ground.'

Louis Gomez (in Herold, 2017)

 ## Learning benefits

Successful use of the approach can develop more independent and confident learners. Students can see the progress they are making and attribute this to their own efforts (Yeh, 2010).

HOW DOES IT WORK?

Approaches to individualisation that use technology suggest two things are important for individualised instruction to be successful. First, the learner needs to be given tasks and feedback (see page 17) at the right level. Second, the pace with which they make progress needs to be greater than they would make in a class setting, with class tasks and class feedback. It is hard to achieve with one teacher and one class. It may be that the teacher's time is spent less effectively in an individualised classroom. The teacher becomes a manager or coordinator rather than an instructor, who demonstrates, models and provides feedback to the class. A high level of challenge may be easier to maintain in a class setting as the teacher can respond to this and adjust with extra support. Too high a level of challenge for 25 pupils all doing different tasks and getting stuck would be impossible to cope with in a lesson. This means pupils tend to be given easier tasks that they can accomplish on their own. This is easier to manage, but it may be too low a level of challenge for learners.

To make individualised learning work in your classroom, follow these five steps for successful implementation:

'Personalized learning's emphasis on offering different content and paths to each student could open the door for watered-down expectations, greater inequities, and more difficulty holding schools accountable.'

Michael Petrilli (in Herold, 2017)

1. Set clear and specific goals.
2. Make sure the goals are challenging but realistic.
3. Check the goals are understood and accepted by the pupil.
4. Ensure the goals are flexible and regularly adapted to progress.
5. Let pupils monitor their own progress too.
6. Encourage pupils to accept greater challenge.

 # Principles

Principle 1: Goldilocks

There are several challenges in getting individualised instruction to work. It can't take too much time to organise and manage, otherwise you may stop doing other valuable things. The learners need to benefit from working on their own. The level of challenge of the tasks and activities must be set just right for each pupil or their time may be wasted.

Principle 2: The Matthew Effect

For individualised instruction to work well, the learners need to be capable of managing their motivation to work on their own and to have a repertoire of skills to tackle challenges when they get stuck. This tends to benefit successful learners who make greater progress. The less motivated and determined learners may get stuck, or work at a slower pace.

Unexpected finding

Individualised instruction is harder to manage than it sounds. All teachers want to meet all of their pupils' needs, but in practice this is more difficult than it seems. Although the average impact is positive, not all approaches to individualising learning have been successful. The teacher's role can become more managerial than instructional and it feels like you are trying to spin 25 plates on 25 poles. If you've ever watched anyone try to do this, they run frantically from pole to pole giving a tiny amount of time to each, spending most of the time running in between.

This may be why approaches that use digital technology can be successful. The tasks and activities are built into the software so you don't have to spend time developing or selecting them. Often learners get quick feedback from the technology to keep them on track. The teacher can then get information from the technology to identify who might be struggling on different topics and provide some focussed teaching to a group who are stuck.

Teaching tips

✓ Focus on efficiency – make sure it's a good use of your pupils' time. They need to be practising and consolidating at an appropriate level. If they are learning new skills or content, they need to have the capability to manage what to do when they get stuck. If they are not motivated and determined, the pace of their work may reduce. If they are practising and consolidating knowledge or skills, check the practice is needed and is effective.

✓ Count the cost of preparing, managing and monitoring all of the different tasks and activities for 25–30 pupils as compared with the efficiency of working with the whole class or a group. Make sure it's a good use of your time!

✓ Use individualised learning in short bursts, perhaps as personal challenges with clear targets for personal improvement so learners can see their own progress over a couple of weeks.

✓ Use it to complement other approaches. For example, you could have one group of pupils working on individualised tasks to provide efficient practice and consolidation, supported by digital technology or by a teaching assistant while you teach another target group more intensively.

Leadership tips

✓ Focus on efficiency – make sure it is a good use of teachers' time. Ensure there is still plenty of time for class and group teaching. It is all too easy for the teacher's time to be taken up with managerial issues.

✓ Identify digital technologies that can help, such as tutorial programs or software that includes diagnosis and feedback to get the level of challenge right. Practice programs in literacy and mathematics can also be effective. Look out for adaptive technologies.

KEY READINGS

Academic

EEF (2018), 'Individualised instruction', *Sutton Trust-EEF Teaching and Learning Toolkit*, https://educationendowmentfoundation.org.uk/evidence-summaries/teaching-learning-toolkit/individualised-instruction/

Ma, W., Adesope, O. O., Nesbit, J. C. and Liu, Q. (2014), 'Intelligent tutoring systems and learning outcomes: A meta-analysis', *Journal of Educational Psychology*, 106, (4), 901.

Yeh, S. S. (2010), 'Understanding and addressing the achievement gap through individualized instruction and formative assessment', *Assessment in Education: Principles, Policy and Practice*, 17, (2), 169–182.

Practical

Pearson, S. (2016), *Rethinking Children and Inclusive Education: Opportunities and complexities*. London: Bloomsbury Academic.

Tod, J., Castle, F. and Blamires, M. (1998), *Individual Education Plans Implementing Effective Practice (IEPs)*. Abingdon: Routledge.

19 COLLABORATIVE LEARNING

WORKING TOGETHER EFFECTIVELY

 Attainment gain   + 5 months   

 Learning benefits
- Improved behaviour and motivation.

 Unexpected finding
- All learners benefit from being taught how to work together.

 Teaching tips
- Start simple.
- Design tasks carefully.
- Use competition carefully.

 Leadership tips
- Offer professional development in these approaches.
- Ensure your record keeping does not undermine collaborative approaches.

 Principles
- Bananarama
- Goldilocks

WHAT IS IT?

A collaborative or cooperative learning approach involves pupils working together on activities or learning tasks in a group small enough for everyone to participate on a collective task that has been clearly assigned and is well structured (Slavin et al., 2003). Pupils in the group work on separate tasks contributing to a common overall outcome, or work together on a shared task with the same outcomes (Gillies, 2016).

> 'Alone we can do so little; together we can do so much.'
>
> **Helen Keller**

Peer tutoring can also be considered as a type of collaborative learning as learners teach each other, but it is included in this book as a separate topic (see page 45).

Some collaborative learning approaches get mixed-capability teams or groups to compete with each other. This uses between-group competition to drive within-group collaboration. There is a wide range of approaches to collaborative and cooperative learning involving different kinds of organisation and tasks. The role of the teacher is crucial here (Buchs et al., 2017), as how you introduce, structure and support collaborative learning affects how pupils respond. It is challenging to get an effective balance between process (working well together) and outcome (learning successfully).

DOES IT WORK?

The impact of collaborative approaches on learning is positive with a typical improvement of five extra months of learning over a year (EEF, 2018g). However, the extent of impact varies, so it is important to get the detail right (Slavin et al., 2003). Effective collaborative learning requires more than sitting pupils together and asking them to work in a group; structured approaches with well-designed tasks lead to the greatest learning gains. There is

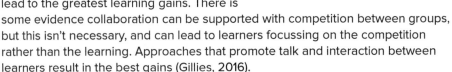

'It is literally true that you can succeed best and quickest by helping others to succeed.'

Oliver Napoleon Hill

some evidence collaboration can be supported with competition between groups, but this isn't necessary, and can lead to learners focussing on the competition rather than the learning. Approaches that promote talk and interaction between learners result in the best gains (Gillies, 2016).

Systematic reviews and meta-analyses provide consistent evidence about the benefits of collaborative learning, for example in literacy (Puzio and Colby, 2013), mathematics (Capar and Tarim, 2015) and science (Romero, 2009). There is also indirect evidence that collaboration can increase the effectiveness of other approaches such as mastery learning (see page 51) or digital technologies (Higgins et al., 2012; see page 83). Collaborative learning works well for all ages if activities are structured for learners' capabilities. It applies across the curriculum. Not all of the specific approaches adopted by schools have been evaluated, so it is important to test out any new initiative.

Learning benefits

Studies report other benefits, from improved social interaction to a better classroom climate. Teachers comment on improved behaviour and motivation. There is a shift in focus for interaction. As learners work together, the teacher can observe and evaluate pupils' current capabilities, working out how to challenge and extend their skills, knowledge and understanding. When working together, pupils regulate each other's behaviour and interaction. The teacher's control is indirect.

HOW DOES IT WORK?

The theory is that in working together learners pool their ideas so they can help each other. They can also think about different ideas in relation to each other and choose the best. Two brains are better than one. We suspect that although this is the case some of the time, most of the time learners working together keep each other on task and engaged. They are not completing significantly harder tasks than they can do on their own; they just get more practice at tasks and activities with about the right level of challenge, and can help each other when they get stuck. This also means the teacher can observe learners talking and making their thinking explicit, providing an excellent opportunity to assess and evaluate what they are doing.

> 'Competition has been shown to be useful up to a certain point and no further, but cooperation, which is the thing we must strive for today, begins where competition leaves off.'
>
> Franklin D. Roosevelt

Principles

Principle 1: Bananarama

Quality is a key principle in collaborative learning. It's how you plan the micro-detail of how learners work together, how they collaborate on the learning content, and how this improves outcomes. Will the tasks increase the amount of learning, because working together keeps pupils on task for longer? Will you set more challenging tasks where the combined effort means learners can succeed together where they couldn't alone? This level of detail in planning is essential.

Principle 2: Goldilocks

Good task design is key. Too easy and it doesn't stretch the group; too hard and they will find it difficult to work together. Find teaching approaches that structure collaboration. These can be simple structures, like 'think, pair, share', or more complex ones, like 'jigsaw groups'. This particular technique makes pupils dependent on each other to succeed. Groups complete activities by undertaking tasks that the group then assembles by putting the (jigsaw) pieces together. It was designed by a social psychologist, Elliot Aronson, to help break down racial tension in schools in the USA that were forcibly integrated (Aronson and Bridgeman, 1979).

The technique splits classes into mixed groups to work on small problems that the group collates into a final outcome. For example, an in-class assignment is divided into topics. Students are then split into groups with one member assigned to each topic. Working individually, each student learns about his or her topic and presents it to their group. Next, students gather into groups divided by topic. Each member presents again to the topic group. In same-topic groups, students reconcile points of view and synthesise information. They create a final report. Finally, the original groups reconvene and listen to presentations from each member. The final presentations provide all group members with an understanding of their own material, as well as the findings that have emerged from topic-specific group discussion. Good organisation and support are essential.

Unexpected finding

All learners benefit from being taught how to work together. You might expect older pupils at the end of primary school or in secondary school to be able to work successfully together, but it is always worth spending some time making expectations clear and getting pupils to practise the specific skills they need to work together well.

Teaching tips

✓ Start simple – use paired and small-group activities first. Pupils need support and practice to work together effectively; it does not happen automatically. Once pupils are used to working together in small groups and with simple structures (such as paired approaches), you can try more complex structures (such as collaborative teams competing against each other or where team roles are assigned).

✓ Tasks need to be designed carefully so that working together is effective and efficient, otherwise some pupils will try to work on their own. This is a reasonable response to a badly designed task.

✓ Use competition carefully. Competition between groups can be used to support pupils in working together more effectively. However, over-emphasis on competition can cause learners to focus on winning rather than succeeding in their learning.

✓ Make sure lower-achieving pupils have the opportunity to talk and articulate their thinking in collaborative tasks to ensure they benefit from the approach. It is all too easy for confident and articulate learners to dominate in group work.

Leadership tips

✓ Professional development is needed to support these approaches. There is a vast array of collaborative task structures for learning. No one will be skilled in using them all. Even when you understand the possibilities, making them work for a particular class and specific learning outcomes is challenging. This needs practice and support, even for experienced teachers.

✓ Ensure your record keeping policies do not undermine collaborative approaches. One group record from a task is enough. You should not expect individual outcomes for every activity.

KEY READINGS

Academic

Capar, G. and Tarim, K. (2015), 'Efficacy of the cooperative learning method on mathematics achievement and attitude: A meta-analysis research', *Educational Sciences: Theory and Practice*, 15, (2), 553–559.

Gillies, R. M. (2016), 'Cooperative learning: Review of research and practice', *Australian Journal of Teacher Education*, 41, (3), 3.

Mercer, N., Dawes, L., Wegerif, R. and Sams, C. (2004), 'Reasoning as a scientist: Ways of helping children to use language to learn science', *British Educational Research Journal*, 30, (3), 359–377.

Slavin, R. E., Hurley, E. A. and Chamberlain, A. (2003), 'Cooperative learning and achievement: Theory and research', in Reynolds, W. M., Miller, G. B. and Weiner, I. B. (eds.), *Handbook of Psychology: Educational psychology* (pp. 177–198). Hoboken, NJ: John Wiley and Sons.

Practical

Dawes, L., Mercer, N. and Wegerif, R. (2000), *Thinking Together: Activities for teachers and children at Key Stage 2*. Birmingham: Questions Publishing Co.

Kagan, M. (2015), *Kagan Cooperative Learning* (revised edn.). San Clemente, CA: Kagan Cooperative Learning.

Slavin, R. E. (2015), 'Cooperative learning in elementary schools', *Education 3–13*, 43, (1), 5–14.

20 SPORTS FOR HEALTH AND WIDER OUTCOMES

 Attainment gain — + 2 months

 Learning benefits
- Better physical and mental health.
- Reduced obesity.
- Improved social skills (e.g. team work).
- Improved attendance.

 Unexpected finding
- Combining sports and academic activities to motivate learners can have a surprising impact.

 Teaching tips
- Activity needs to be regular and of at least moderate intensity.
- Young children need the chance to move frequently and vigorously.

 Leadership tips
- Ensure you meet your pupils' physical as well as intellectual needs.

 Principles
- Bananarama

WHAT IS IT?

The research on sports participation and interventions to increase physical activity have often been seen as a means to boost engagement and attainment at school. This might be through organised after-school activities or a programme run by a local sporting club or association. Sometimes sporting activity is used as a means to encourage young people to engage in extra learning activities, such as football training at a local football club combined with study skills, literacy, computer or mathematics lessons. This misses the point.

> 'Orandum est ut sit mens sana in corpore sano.' [You should pray for a healthy mind in a healthy body.]
>
> **Juvenal**

We need children and young people to be physically active for more important reasons than their mathematics test scores (important though these are).

DOES IT WORK?

The overall impact of sports participation and physical activity on academic achievement tends to be positive but low (about two extra months' progress; Singh et al., 2012) for both primary (de Greeff et al., 2018) and secondary (Trudeau and Shephard, 2008) pupils.

Evidence from the UK shows sports participation can have a larger effect on, for example, mathematics learning but only when combined with structured numeracy teaching. One study shows an impact of up to ten months' extra progress; Schucan-Bird et al., 2013). In this circumstance the 'participation' acted as an incentive to undertake extra instruction. The quality of the programme and the link that is made with academic learning may make more difference than the specific type of approach or sporting activities involved.

Learning benefits

The more physical activity, the greater the health benefits. The NHS (2018) in the UK recommend that children should do at least 60 minutes of activity every day. Exercise should be of at least a moderate intensity. That said, benefits can be achieved through 30 minutes of activity per day – particularly for children at high risk of obesity. Something is better than nothing. Team sport is associated with improved social interaction, social skills and confidence, perhaps due to the social nature of the participation. It also offers opportunities to develop leadership skills and an understanding of strategy and tactics. There are things to watch out for, such as ensuring healthy growth: some sports can develop muscle and bone development on one side of the body, such as in tennis or single-oar rowing. Other risks such as concussion in sports like rugby can be avoided with non-contact rules.

Sport and exercise as currently practised in schools aren't a panacea for healthier lives, however. Children taking part in sport don't always enjoy wholesome diets. They were found to consume more fruit and vegetables, but also more fast food and sugary drinks. It is unclear whether current practice protects young people from becoming overweight.

We need to up our game – both in the physical exercise and sport we offer our school children, but also in the rigorous research required to elucidate clearer causal links between activities and their many likely positive outcomes.

HOW DOES IT WORK?

The main mechanism seems to be through enhanced confidence or the increased practice motivated by the opportunity to be involved in sporting activities. The mechanisms for impact on other subjects (known as 'transfer' in the psychological literature) are not well understood (see arts participation, page 119). Some recent research suggests that learning to control your own attention and focus on what you are doing may be an important generalisable ability (Greenwood and Parasuraman, 2016).

'Physical fitness is not only one of the most important keys to a healthy body, it is the basis of dynamic and creative intellectual activity.'

John F. Kennedy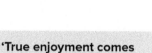

 Principles

Principle 1: Bananarama

There is considerable variation in the impact that sports participation and physical activity have on academic outcomes. This suggests the quality of the programme and the link made with academic learning is more important than the specific type of approach or sporting activities involved.

'True enjoyment comes from activity of the mind and exercise of the body; the two are ever united.'

Wilhelm von Humboldt

If you are interested in the wider educational benefits of sports in terms of developing collaborative skills, using strategies or leadership skills, as well as the physical benefits, then sports participation alone is likely to be sufficient. If you are interested in improvements in specific subjects like literacy or mathematics, you may need to think about how to develop the connection or use the participation to drive increased practice, such as through motivation.

Unexpected finding

Combining sports and academic activities to motivate learners can have a surprising impact. One study found as much as ten months' improvement resulting from the combination of sports and intensive teaching (Schucan-Bird et al., 2013).

Teaching tips

✓ Activity for all pupils needs to be regular and of at least moderate intensity. Children and young people benefit physically and developmentally from regular exercise. Build it into the school timetable.

✓ Ensure young children get the chance to move frequently and vigorously to develop muscle and bone growth as well as to develop habits to form a healthy lifestyle.

✓ Make specific links between strategies to succeed in sports and strategies in other subjects.

✓ Collaborative skills are essential in many team games; again, making the links explicit or using some of the language from sports as metaphors in more academic learning can be a useful way to develop the connection.

Leadership tips

✓ Ensure you meet your pupils' physical as well as intellectual needs. Schools have an important part to play in educating their pupils and developing effective habits in relation to both academic work and physical exercise.

✓ There are a number of organisations and charities that will help with school sports and you don't always need your own facilities.

✓ Regular walking or jogging can be a good way to get started. See https://thedailymile.co.uk.

KEY READINGS

Academic

Schucan-Bird, K., Tripney, J. and Newman, M. (2013), 'The educational impacts of young people's participation in organised sport: A systematic review', *Journal of Children's Services*, 8, (4), 264–275.

Trudeau, F. and Shephard, R. J. (2008), 'Physical education, school physical activity, school sports and academic performance', *International Journal of Behavioral Nutrition and Physical Activity*, 5, (1), 10.

Practical

John, M. F. (2000), *Book of Simple Songs Circles: Wonderful songs and rhymes passed down from generation to generation*. Chicago: GIA Publications.

Mosley, J. (2009), *Jenny Mosley's Top 100 Playground Games to Enjoy SEAL Outside*. Hyde: LDA.

Rose, J. (2017), *Bloomsbury Curriculum Basics: Teaching Primary PE*. London: Bloomsbury Education.

Stidder, G. and Hayes, S. (2016), *The Really Useful Physical Education Book*. Abingdon: Routledge.

21 ART FOR ART'S SAKE

Attainment gain	+ 2 months	
Learning benefits	• Increased motivation. • Greater self-confidence. • Learning outcomes in art-based subjects.	
Unexpected finding	• Learning to play a musical instrument is a valuable skill in itself, but also appears to raise educational attainment.	
Teaching tips	• Link arts activities with other curriculum areas. • Find an expert who can help.	
Leadership tips	• Resist the pressure to narrow the curriculum. • Develop expertise in a few selected areas. • Maintain engagement for vulnerable pupils through arts approaches.	
Principles	• The Matthew Effect • Bananarama	

WHAT IS IT?

Arts participation is involvement in artistic and creative activities, such as dance, drama, music, painting, drawing or sculpture across a range of media (EEF, 2018h). This can be as part of the curriculum or as extra-curricular activities organised by the school or by parents. Arts participation could be through a regular weekly or monthly activity, or it might be through more intensive programmes such as summer schools or residential courses.

These activities have important educational value in themselves. They should be valued as part of the wider curriculum, rather than just a means of improving test scores. A broad and balanced curriculum is important both for individual children who can succeed across a wide range of outcomes from schooling, but also for wider society in terms of how we prepare our children and young people for the world outside school.

> 'Art washes from the soul the dust of everyday life.'
>
> **Pablo Picasso**

DOES IT WORK?

Important wider outcomes such as more positive attitudes to learning and increased self-confidence and wellbeing have been reported with arts-based approaches (Secker et al., 2007). This is especially from music, where learning to play an instrument is associated with better educational attainment. Other similar outcomes are reported from activities like drama and developing fine arts and craft skills as well as digital arts (such as digital design, photography and film-making).

Some arts activities have been linked with improvements in specific academic outcomes. For example, there is evidence of a positive link between music and spatial awareness (Hallam, 2015) and between drama and writing (Lee et al., 2015). Choral singing has positive effects on wellbeing and emotional resilience (Gridley et al., 2011).

Overall, the impact of various kinds of arts participation on academic learning is positive but low. Arts interventions have educational value in themselves, but they are not, on average, a particularly effective way to raise academic attainment in other subjects. That said, improved outcomes have been identified in English, mathematics and science. Benefits have been found in both primary and secondary schools, with greater effects on average for younger learners and, in some cases, for disadvantaged pupils. Wider benefits such as more positive attitudes to learning and increased wellbeing have been reported (Catterall, 2012).

Participation and engagement in creative and arts-based activities should be an important feature of education. In recent years we have seen a narrowing of the curriculum and a reduction in the range of art-based subjects offered for examination at secondary school. We need to consider the kind of society we aspire to foster for the next generation. Do we want a narrow but efficient range of subjects for all, or do we want to support a breadth of expertise and success across a wealth of subjects, which includes music, fine arts and drama? What would schooling look like if we valued English and mathematics for the value that they added to art and music achievement?

Learning benefits

Some arts activities have been linked with improvements in specific academic subjects and other areas. For example, there is evidence of a positive link between music and spatial awareness (Hallam, 2015) and between drama and writing (Lee et al., 2015). Choral singing has positive effects on wellbeing and emotional resilience (Gridley et al., 2011).

HOW DOES IT WORK?

As with sports participation (see page 115) the main mechanism seems to be through enhanced confidence and the development of particular skills (such as speaking and listening in drama or the development of fine motor skills in music and fine arts). The mechanisms for impact on other subjects (known as 'transfer' in the psychological literature) are not well understood, though recent research suggests that learning to control your own attention and focus on what you are doing may be an important generalisable ability (Greenwood and Parasuraman, 2016).

'We share the importance of the arts, not only in society but also in building one's self-esteem. And the kids really grasp that: They're confident and proud of themselves and share art with the people in their lives.'

Agnes Gund,
Founder of Studio
in a School

Principles

Principle 1: The Matthew Effect

'To those who have shall more be given' is particularly appropriate for arts participation. Children and young people from advantaged backgrounds are more likely to have these experiences, either through the schools they attend or provided by their parents in after-school lessons and clubs. It is important that schools in less advantaged areas provide these opportunities for their pupils.

Principle 2: Bananarama

If your goal is to support academic achievement in other subjects then you will need to be clear how you think this will work. The evidence shows a wide range of effects from the programmes and approaches studied. What is the link between your chosen arts intervention and the outcomes you want to improve, and how will you tell if it's successful? Are you looking for increased motivation or greater self-esteem and self-regulation? Decide what your objective is, then find an intervention that aims to deliver it. Regularly measure progress to check the intervention is having the desired impact.

Unexpected finding

Learning to play an instrument is a valuable skill in itself, but has wider benefits. Many studies show direct and indirect benefits from learning to play a musical instrument (Benz et al., 2016), such as in reading (Standley, 2008) and reasoning (Forgeard et al., 2008). It is hard to tell exactly how the effects arise, whether this is from learning to read musical notation, from the physical motor skills developed in playing, or from greater confidence and enjoyment.

Teaching tips

✓ Link arts activities with other curriculum areas. From time to time, either as a class project or a school project, work together on a theme or topic through which you can celebrate achievement with an exhibition, a performance or a show.

✓ Find an expert who can help. Unless you are lucky enough to be exceptionally talented, it is unlikely you will have the skills yourself to teach across the whole of the arts. How can you bring expertise into your classroom – through volunteers, older students, a local club or university students? It is important to be fully involved yourself though. Use it as an opportunity for professional development.

Leadership tips

✓ Resist the pressure to narrow the curriculum. Decide what your vision is for a broader perspective on educational achievement than English and mathematics (essential though these are). What can you achieve through the curriculum, and where might you want to extend this through extra-curricular activities?

✓ Develop expertise in a few selected areas. Don't try to cover everything. Identify some areas of potential achievement for pupils at your school and pursue these. Can you build links with other organisations or encourage extra-curricular activities? It may take some work to get these up and running, but once in place they should be easier to maintain.

✓ Maintain engagement for vulnerable pupils through arts approaches. Arts-based approaches may offer a route to re-engage older or more vulnerable pupils in learning. It can provide opportunities for achievement or just a neutral space in which to build up relationships.

KEY READINGS

Academic

Hallam, S. (2015), *The Power of Music: A research synthesis of the impact of actively making music on the intellectual, social and personal development of children and young people*. London: International Music Education Research Centre (iMerc).

Lee, B. K., Patall, E. A., Cawthon, S. W. and Steingut, R. R. (2015), 'The effect of drama-based pedagogy on pre K–16 outcomes: A meta-analysis of research from 1985 to 2012', *Review of Educational Research*, 85, (1), 3–49.

OECD (2013), *Art for Art's Sake? The impact of arts education*. Paris: OECD.

Practical

Atkinson, R. (2018), *Mastering Primary Music*. London: Bloomsbury Academic.

Daubney, A. (2017), *Teaching Primary Music*. London: Sage.

Farmer, D. and Hurtado, D. (2011), *Learning Through Drama in the Primary Years*. Self-published.

Gopaul, E. (2017), *Bloomsbury Curriculum Basics: Teaching Primary Art and Design*. London: Bloomsbury Education.

AFTERWORD: A FINAL PRINCIPLE

Campbell's Law: Reforming testing to promote equity and evidence

The words that have come to be known as Campbell's Law were written in a seminal 1979 research paper detailing the best ways of evaluating programmes attempting social change (Campbell, 1979). Donald T. Campbell argued that a simple statistical indicator used to measure a complex organisation is doomed to become unreliable as it distorts the behaviour of the people it's intended to measure. To put it more simply, anything that is measured and rewarded will be gamed (Muller, 2018).

'The more any quantitative social indicator is used for social decision-making, the more subject it will be to corruption pressures,' wrote Campbell. 'And the more apt it will be to distort and corrupt the social processes it is intended to monitor.' Campbell added, 'When test scores become the goal of the teaching process, they both lose their value as indicators of educational status and distort the educational process in undesirable ways.'

Forty years on, Campbell's Law manifests itself in myriad ways in the modern era of management performance metrics. Police forces record fewer incidents as crimes to make it look like their district is getting safer. Surgeons opt out of tricky operations for fear of lowering their hospital success rates. Academics obsess over research citations at the expense of impacting on the real world (Wilsdon et al., 2015). Campbell's Law is closely related to Goodhart's Law named after the economist Charles Goodhart. Goodhart argued that when a measure becomes a target, it ceases to be a good measure (Strathern, 1997).

Britain has led the world in the drive to use metrics (see for example Barber et al., 2011) and nowhere has succumbed more to metrification than our school system. Schools are held to account by reams of published achievement and progress data on their children. Perceived poor performance can trigger visits from school inspectors and the possibility of being placed in special measures. The logic is that by demanding high standards, measured by test scores, schools will teach their pupils better. Those who fail to do so are exposed and penalised.

But this edifice is built on heroic assumptions that simple statistics can be robust and reliable measures of learning. Academic standards are only as good as the tests they are based on. Examinations reflect only part of the curriculum. Add to this the unrealistic expectations that schools are capable of addressing all of society's ills, and it's the perfect breeding ground for Campbell's Law. High-stakes accountability narrows the school curriculum, distorts what teachers teach and undermines confidence in the end-of-year tests on which it rests.

An emaciated curriculum

Extra time devoted to preparing for English, mathematics and traditional academic disciplines prioritised in league tables has squeezed out subjects like music, art, languages and physical education (Harford, 2017). Children are removed from lessons for reading and writing interventions and exam preparation. Many schools in England start GCSE courses a year earlier to meet the growing demands of the exams – narrowing the curriculum for children at an earlier age. Many pupils don't study history, geography or a language after the age of 13. In the United States, this trend has been called 'goal diversion' (Muller, 2018). It has prompted accusations that we are producing 'factory-farmed' children devoid of the skills deemed important by employers – problem solving, critical thinking and creativity (Teaching Times, 2018). As we have already argued, it means pupils miss out on the life enhancing impact of art and sport – benefits not easily captured in simple statistics.

Cross-curricular themes and life skills slip between the cracks. Politicians then try to jemmy them back into the curricular ecology in special lessons, monitored through the blunt instrument of school inspections. We rarely consider the opportunity cost of marginal gains in tested achievement, and the collateral damage they cause to the curriculum.

Narrowing within subjects

There has also been a narrowing of what children are taught within subjects. Teachers focus on the topics of the subject that are tested and ignore those that are not. Activities that don't appear on the test are pushed back to the end of the school year, or disappear from the curriculum entirely.

The problem is that narrowly focussed tests and mark schemes benefit from being reliable – consistently ranking which students get the best marks each year. But this doesn't make them valid, as they cover a limited range of topics in a subject. The reliability and validity of tests are two distinct features of the exam system. You can understand the difference by considering the example of bathroom scales. A scale is reliable if it registers the same weight each time you step on it. But this doesn't mean it is giving a valid or accurate measurement. It may be consistently misjudging your weight as heavier or lighter than it actually is. It is only valid if it shows your true weight.

The high-stakes testing system is founded on reliable but increasingly invalid assessments. This is because high-stakes tests are primarily about comparing changing standards. What makes this dangerous is that the assessment process appears to be functioning well – consistently producing test scores – but the compromises being made aren't immediately apparent. Average test scores rise each year and are heralded as evidence of improved standards, but the quality and breadth of education children receive is likely to have declined. The scales are consistently overestimating the weight of knowledge and learning gained.

Shallow learning – teaching to the test

High-stakes testing has also distorted pedagogy itself – how teachers go about their classroom practice. Unrelenting pressure to do well in tests shifts teaching towards demonstrating performance, rather than promoting broader knowledge, understanding and capability. Pupils are prepared and practised to answer examination questions so all of the marks they can score on the assessment rubric are ticked in their answer. Teaching to the test comes at a cost – meaning less time for developing meaning and content, creativity and breadth of knowledge.

The distorting effects of Campbell's Law not only distract teachers from genuine improvements in learning but take up huge costs, in time and resources, in the pursuit of inflating test scores. England's school inspectorate, Ofsted, found that many primary schools were getting children to repeat reading comprehension tests, rather than reading a wide range of books (Ofsted, 2019). Shallow learning from teaching to the test is particularly acute among UK pupils (Vaughan, 2015).

Cheating

Amid mounting pressures on schools to secure the best test results, a minority can't resist the temptation to stretch the rules or abandon them altogether. What makes this doubly unfair is that in our zero-sum assessment regime, one extra grade won through foul means by one pupil means a grade dropped for another innocent pupil elsewhere.

Loopholes often arise from well-meaning measures. Children who are diagnosed as having dyslexia and dyspraxia, for example, are given extra time for their exams. But research for the BBC found one in five students in private schools had received extra time to complete tests – compared with one in eight pupils in state schools (Bateman, 2017). Gaining 25 per cent more time when sitting high-stakes end-of-year tests is a huge advantage. Exam regulators now ask whether schools are gaming the system or responding to genuine learning difficulties.

Another tactic is to off-roll students – excluding poorly performing pupils ahead of GCSE exams so they don't harm a school's performance. An Ofsted investigation found that thousands of pupils had been encouraged to leave schools, failing to appear on school registers elsewhere (Bradbury, 2018). 'It's almost certainly to help the school because the most disruptive, hardest to teach children are likely to be the ones who will have the worst progress scores, so by losing them you are likely to be bringing up your school results,' Chief inspector Amanda Spielman told *The Times* (Sylvester and Thomson, 2018).

As the pressure for year-on-year improvements ratchets up, more schools have crossed the line completely. A rising number have been investigated for cheating during exams and found to have committed 'malpractice offences' (Perraudin, 2018). Teachers have been caught helping students in their exams – termed 'improper assistance' or 'over-aiding'. Students are more likely to cheat in classes that emphasise tests and grades (Anderman, 2018).

Cheating is observed throughout the system. A Government inquiry was launched to investigate after teachers at leading public schools were accused of passing information to pupils about their upcoming exams (Yorke, 2017). The scandal prompted resignations and calls for tighter rules under which teachers work as examiners writing and reviewing question papers. A small number of cases these may be, but they are rising with each year.

Implications for equity and evidence

The distorting impact of Campbell's Law is a threat to both equity and evidence in education. Pupils from disadvantaged homes face a double whammy. The system creates strong incentives for schools to be socially selective in their admissions – the biggest single influence on their headline scores is the achievement of pupils they attract to the school in the first place. Schools ranked highly in league tables have far smaller proportions of children on free school meals than the rates of FSM pupils in the local surrounding areas (Sutton Trust, 2005). Poorer pupils can be victims of the relentless pressures on schools serving mixed communities – restricted in their subject choice or off-rolled from the school altogether.

Our fear is that crude high-stakes accountability will only exacerbate the attainment gap. In this book we highlight several approaches that can push back against education's prevailing wind, but they are not quick or easy fixes. Social mobility can't be done on the cheap. A recurring message is to not underestimate the time and resources needed by teachers to deliver evidence-informed practice. If you want to maximise your chances of delivering best bets in the classroom, you need to work hard on what has worked.

The pressure from high-stakes accountability leaves little time for research engagement in the classroom. Leaders in schools might believe that research and evidence are important, but are forced to prioritise more immediate accountability concerns and are nervous about adding an extra burden onto busy teachers (Coldwell et al., 2017). The immediate pressures have put paid to risk-taking, cooperation with other schools and long-term reflective practice.

Teacher-led assessment

How do we rid the system of these unintended consequences? It's not by doing away with tests altogether, but by rebalancing the assessment regime.

An evidence-informed education system requires teachers to be empowered as professional assessors – trained to measure deeper learning, higher-level skills and a range of knowledge among their pupils. Classroom tests should be formative in nature, complementing external summative tests. As John Hattie (2008) argues in his book *Visible Learning*, 'teachers need to be evaluators of the effect of the methods that they choose'.

Our plea is that teachers assess and evaluate whatever they choose to do: setting clear goals, being clear how they aim to achieve them and knowing how they will measure success. What progress are you expecting and what counts as success? That's the corollary to all the best bets and advice we've compiled in this book: what works in your school, or your classroom, for your pupils?

We need a mix of tests: some instigated by teachers as an integral part of their teaching and learning to measure progress of their pupils in class; some deployed by researchers to track outcomes of trials looking at different school approaches; and others used by external bodies to monitor education standards in their broadest sense.

Ideally, this would be a bottom-up and top-down regime – where metrics are used to aid professional practice and assess children's progress. Too often tests are part of an education system that is done to teachers, not shaped by them. Curriculum and pedagogy should be developed by teachers, not dictated by test and textbook publishers. The challenge would be to do all this without increasing the total amount of testing.

If it comes to a choice, validity in assessments for improving classroom practice is more important than their reliability. We would rather have a bathroom scale that reveals our true weight than one that consistently gives the faulty impression of progress being made. This would help drive practice in schools towards learning, rather than performance. We prioritise assessment of learning over assessment for learning. A better balance between the two is required. Measures with greater reliability would be reserved for research trials. They could also be used for national sampling of standards of performance over time. School inspections would assess the quality and diversity of assessment in schools as well as their curriculum offer. If league tables are to remain, let's make them one part of a more balanced assessment regime.

We are often asked what a national policy for promoting evidence in education should look like. Campbell's Law has been found to operate at this 'meta-level' as well. Attempts to establish an evidence-based policy by the New Labour Government of the late 1990s ended up producing corrupted data to defend its record, according to at least one analysis. The Government pursued research to support policies already decided upon. This was 'policy-based evidence' rather than evidence-based policy (Boden and Epstein, 2006).

A national policy for evidence-informed teaching is about creating the conditions for research use in the classroom, not telling teachers what to do from on high. At the policy level, you need to be confident that the effects of a recommended approach are consistent and that the impact is high. Otherwise you risk reducing the effectiveness of the best teachers as you improve the practice of those less effective: a policy in which everyone regresses to the mean and there is no overall improvement.

We need to adopt an expertise model of teaching, where evidence for a particular goal and information about a particular class are used to inform professional judgement about where improvement can be achieved.

A broad and balanced curriculum is important both for individual children who can succeed across a wide range of outcomes from schooling, but also for wider society in terms of how we prepare our children and young people for the world outside of school. We want an education system that promotes fluency in reading, writing and mathematical capability for children from all backgrounds, but not at the cost of depth of learning in high-stakes subjects, the evaporation of other important subjects from the timetable, and the diminishing of evidence-informed practice in the classroom.

REFERENCES

Anderman, E. M. (2018), 'Why students at prestigious high schools still cheat on exams', *The Conversation*, https://theconversation.com/why-students-at-prestigious-high-schools-still-cheat-on-exams-91041

Andrews, J., Robinson, D. and Hutchinson, J. (2017), 'Closing the gap? Trends in educational attainment and disadvantage'. London: Education Policy Institute. https://epi.org.uk/publications-and-research/closing-gap-trends-educational-attainment-disadvantage/

Aronson, E. and Bridgeman, D. (1979), 'Jigsaw groups and the desegregated classroom: In pursuit of common goals', *Personality and Social Psychology Bulletin*, 5, (4), 438–446.

Askew, M., Brown, M., Rhodes, V., Wiliam, D. and Johnson, D. (1997), 'Effective teachers of numeracy: Report of a study carried out for the Teacher Training Agency'. London: King's College, University of London.

Aslaksen, K. and Lorås, H. (2018), 'The modality-specific learning style hypothesis: A mini-review', *Frontiers in Psychology*, 9, 1538.

Bandura, A. (1982), 'Self-efficacy mechanism in human agency', *American Psychologist*, 37, (2), 122–147.

Barber, M., Kihn, P. and Moffit, A. (2011), 'Deliverology: From idea to implementation'. London; Washington, DC: McKinsey & Company, www.mckinsey.com/~/media/mckinsey/dotcom/client_service/Public%20Sector/PDFS/McK%20on%20Govt/Change%20under%20pressure/TG_MoG_6_Deliverology.ashx

Bateman, T. (2017), 'Independent school students gain extra time for exams', *BBC News*, www.bbc.co.uk/news/education-38923034

Baye, A., Inns, A., Lake, C. and Slavin, R. E. (2019), 'A synthesis of quantitative research on reading programs for secondary students', *Reading Research Quarterly*, 54, (2), 133–166.

Benz, S., Sellaro, R., Hommel, B. and Colzato, L. S. (2016), 'Music makes the world go round: The impact of musical training on non-musical cognitive functions—A review', *Frontiers in Psychology*, 6, 2023.

Biesta, G. (2007), 'Why "what works" won't work: Evidence-based practice and the democratic deficit in educational research', *Educational Theory*, 57, (1), 1–22.

Bjork, E. L. and Bjork, R. A. (2011), 'Making things hard on yourself, but in a good way: Creating desirable difficulties to enhance learning', in M. A. Gernsbacher, R. W. Pew and L. M. Hough (eds.), *Psychology and the Real World: Essays illustrating fundamental contributions to society*. New York, NY: Worth Publishers (pp. 56–64). http://bjorklab.psych.ucla.edu/pubs/EBjork_RBjork_2011.pdf

Black, P. and Wiliam, D. (1998), 'Assessment and classroom learning', *Assessment in Education: Principles, Policy and Practice*, 5, (1), 7–74.

Black, P. and Wiliam, D. (2010), 'Inside the black box: Raising standards through classroom assessment', *Phi Delta Kappan*, 92, (1), 81–90.

Black, P., Harrison, C., Hodgen, J., Marshall, B. and Serret, N. (2011), 'Can teachers' summative assessments produce dependable results and also enhance classroom learning?', *Assessment in Education: Principles, Policy and Practice*, 18, (4), 451–469.

Blake, W. (1793), *The Marriage of Heaven and Hell*.

Blatchford, P., Bassett, P., Brown, P., Martin, C., Russell, A. and Webster, R. (2009), 'Deployment and impact of support staff project'. London: Department for Children, Schools and Families. http://maximisingtas.co.uk/assets/content/dissressum.pdf

Blatchford, P., Russell, A., Bassett, P., Brown, P. and Martin, C. (2007), 'The role and effects of teaching assistants in English primary schools (Years 4 to 6) 2000–2003. Results from the Class Size and Pupil–Adult Ratios (CSPAR) KS2 Project', *British Educational Research Journal*, 33, (1), 5–26.

Block, J. (1971), *Mastery Learning: Theory and practice*. New York, NY: Holt, Rinehart & Winston.

Bloom, B. S. (1968), 'Learning for mastery', *Evaluation Comment*, 1, (2), 1–12.

Bloom, B. S. (1980), 'The new direction in educational research: Alterable variables', *The Phi Delta Kappan*, 61, (6), 382–385.

Bloom, B. S. (1984), 'The 2 sigma problem: The search for methods of group instruction as effective as one-to-one tutoring', *Educational Researcher*, 13, (6), 4–16.

Boden, A., Archwamety, T. and McFarland, M. (2000), 'Programmed instruction in secondary education: A meta-analysis of the impact of class size on its effectiveness', paper presented at the Annual Meeting of the National Association of School Psychologists (New Orleans, LA, March 28 – April 1, 2000).

Boden, R. and Epstein, D. (2006), 'Managing the research imagination? Globalisation and research in higher education', *Globalisation, Societies and Education*, 4, (2), 223–236.

BPS Research Digest (2018), 'An extra reason to abandon learning styles – teachers and pupils do not agree on the pupils' preferred learning style', https://digest.bps.org.uk/2018/12/12/an-additional-reason-to-abandon-learning-stylesteachers-and-pupils-do-not-agree-on-the-pupils-preferred-learning-style/

Bradbury, J. (2018), 'Off-rolling: using data to see a fuller picture', *Ofsted Blog*, https://educationinspection.blog.gov.uk/2018/06/26/off-rolling-using-data-to-see-a-fuller-picture/

Bradbury B., Corak, M., Waldfogel, J. and Washbrook, E. (2015), *Too Many Children Left Behind: The U.S. achievement gap in comparative perspective*. New York, NY: Russell Sage Foundation.

Brown, M., Askew, M., Rhodes, V., Denvir, H., Ranson, E. and Wiliam, D. (2001), 'Magic bullets or chimeras? Searching for factors characterising effective teachers and effective teaching in numeracy', BERA Annual Conference, Leeds, www.ncetm.org.uk/public/files/29311/Brown%25253DAskew_BERA01_chimeras.pdf

Brown, V., Crawford, C., Dearden, L., Greaves, E., Kitchen, S., Payne, C., Purdon, S. and Tanner, E. (2012), 'Evaluation of the free school meals pilot: Impact report'. London: Department for Education.

Buchs, C., Filippou, D., Pulfrey, C. and Volpé, Y. (2017), 'Challenges for cooperative learning implementation: Reports from elementary school teachers', *Journal of Education for Teaching*, 43, (3), 296–306.

Burnim, K. O. (2012), 'The importance of phonics in early childhood education', *ABC Mouse*, www.abcmouse.com/newsletter/phonics

Cabinet Office (2013), 'What Works Network', www.gov.uk/guidance/what-works-network

Campbell, D. T. (1979), 'Assessing the impact of planned social change', *Evaluation and Program Planning*, 2, (1), 67–90.

Canadian Council on Learning (2009), 'Homework helps, but not always', https://eric.ed.gov/?id=ED519297

Capar, G. and Tarim, K. (2015), 'Efficacy of the cooperative learning method on mathematics achievement and attitude: A meta-analysis research', *Educational Sciences: Theory and Practice*, 15, (2), 553–559.

Carden, J. and Cline, T. (2015), 'Problem solving in mathematics: The significance of visualisation and related working memory', *Educational Psychology in Practice*, 31, (3), 235–246.

Catterall, J. S. (2012), 'The arts and achievement in at-risk youth: Findings from four longitudinal studies. Research report # 55'. Washington, DC: National Endowment for the Arts.

Cobley, S., Abraham, C. and Baker, J. (2008), 'Relative age effects on physical education attainment and school sport representation', *Physical Education and Sport Pedagogy*, 13, (3), 267–276.

Cockburn, I., Fisher, A., Mansell, E., Thind, A. and Phillips, T. (2015), 'Funding for disadvantaged pupils'. London: National Audit Office. www.nao.org.uk/wp-content/uploads/2015/06/Survey-evidence-from-pupils-parents-and-school-leaders.pdf

Coe, R. (2014), 'Classroom observation: it's harder than you think', www.cem.org/blog/414/

Coe, R., Aloisi, C., Higgins, S. and Major, L. E. (2014), 'What makes great teaching?'. London: Sutton Trust. www.suttontrust.com/wp-content/uploads/2014/10/What-Makes-Great-Teaching-REPORT.pdf

Cohen, P. A., Kulik, J. A. and Kulik, C. C. (1982), 'Education outcomes of tutoring: A meta-analysis of findings', *American Educational Research Journal*, 19, 237–248.

Coldwell, M., Greany, T., Higgins, S., Brown, C., Maxwell, B., Stiell, B., Stoll, L., Willis, B. and Burns, H. (2017), 'Evidence-informed teaching: An evaluation of progress in England'. London: Department for Education. www.gov.uk/government/publications/evidence-informed-teaching-evaluation-of-progress-in-england

Connor, C. M., Morrison, F. J., Fishman, B., Crowe, E. C., Al Otaiba, S. and Schatschneider, C. (2013), 'A longitudinal cluster-randomized controlled study on the accumulating effects of individualized literacy instruction on students' reading from first through third grade', *Psychological Science*, 24, (8), 1408–1419.

Cooper, H., Robinson, J. C. and Patall, E. A. (2006), 'Does homework improve academic achievement? A synthesis of research, 1987–2003', *Review of Educational Research*, 76, (1), 1–62.

Coyne, M. D., Zipoli Jr, R. P., Chard, D. J., Faggella-Luby, M., Ruby, M., Santoro, L. E., and Baker, S. (2009), 'Direct instruction of comprehension: Instructional examples from intervention research on listening and reading comprehension', *Reading and Writing Quarterly*, 25, (2–3), 221–245.

Crawford, C., Dearden, L. and Greaves, E. (2013), 'When you are born matters: Evidence for England', *IFS Reports* (No. R80). London: Institute for Fiscal Studies.

Cuban, L. (1993). 'Computers meet classroom: Classroom wins', *Teachers College Record*, 95, (2), 185–210.

D'Agostino, J. V. and Harmey, S. J. (2016), 'An international meta-analysis of Reading Recovery', *Journal of Education for Students Placed at Risk (JESPAR)*, 21, (1), 29–46.

de Greeff, J. W., Bosker, R. J., Oosterlaan, J., Visscher, C. and Hartman, E. (2018), 'Effects of physical activity on executive functions, attention and academic performance in preadolescent children: A meta-analysis', *Journal of Science and Medicine in Sport*, 21, (5), 501–507.

Department for Education (2010a), 'Government announces pupil premium to raise achievement', www.gov.uk/government/news/government-announces-pupil-premium-to-raise-achievement

Department for Education (2010b), 'New endowment fund to turn around weakest schools and raise standards for disadvantaged pupils', www.gov.uk/government/news/new-endowment-fund-to-turn-around-weakest-schools-and-raise-standards-for-disadvantaged-pupils

Dewald, J. F., Meijer, A. M., Oort, F. J., Kerkhof, G. A. and Bögels, S. M. (2010), 'The influence of sleep quality, sleep duration and sleepiness on school performance in children and adolescents: A meta-analytic review', *Sleep Medicine Reviews*, 14, (3), 179–189.

Dewey, J. (1916), *Democracy and Education: An introduction to the philosophy of education*. New York, NY: Macmillan.

Dunlosky, J., Rawson, K. A., Marsh, E. J., Nathan, M. J., Willingham, D. T. (2013), 'Improving students' learning with effective learning techniques: Promising directions from cognitive and educational psychology', *Psychological Science in the Public Interest*, 14, (1), 4–58, www.indiana.edu/~pcl/rgoldsto/courses/dunloskyimprovinglearning.pdf

Dweck, C. S. (1999), 'Caution – praise can be dangerous', *American Educator*, www.aft.org/sites/default/files/periodicals/PraiseSpring99.pdf

Dweck, C. (2016), 'What having a "growth mindset" actually means', *Harvard Business Review*, 13.

Dweck, C. S. (2017), *Mindset: Changing the way you think to fulfil your potential* (revised edn.). New York, NY: Random House.

Easton, M. (2014), 'Learning the facts about learning', *BBC News*, www.bbc.co.uk/news/uk-30210514?SThisFB

Edison, T. (1913), Interview for *The New York Dramatic Mirror*, July.

EEF (2015), 'Mastery learning: Technical appendix', *Sutton Trust-EEF Teaching and Learning Toolkit*, https://educationendowmentfoundation.org.uk/evidence-summaries/teaching-learning-toolkit/mastery-learning/technical-appendix

EEF (2016), 'Evidence on marking', https://educationendowmentfoundation.org.uk/evidence-summaries/on-marking/

EEF (2017a), 'Peer tutoring in secondary schools', https://educationendowmentfoundation.org.uk/projects-and-evaluation/projects/peer-tutoring-in-secondary-schools/

EEF (2017b), 'Feedback and monitoring pupil progress', https://educationendowmentfoundation.org.uk/school-themes/feedback-monitoring-pupil-progress/

EEF (2017c), 'Physically Active Lessons', https://educationendowmentfoundation.org.uk/projects-and-evaluation/projects/physically-active-lessons/

EEF (2018a), 'Social and emotional learning', *Sutton Trust-EEF Teaching and Learning Toolkit*, https://educationendowmentfoundation.org.uk/evidence-summaries/teaching-learning-toolkit/social-and-emotional-learning/

EEF (2018b), 'Tutor Trust: Affordable primary tuition: Evaluation report and executive summary', https://educationendowmentfoundation.org.uk/public/files/Projects/Evaluation_Reports/Tutor_Trust.pdf

EEF (2018c), 'One to one tuition', *Sutton Trust-EEF Teaching and Learning Toolkit*, https://educationendowmentfoundation.org.uk/evidence-summaries/teaching-learning-toolkit/one-to-one-tuition/

EEF (2018d), 'Homework (primary)', *Sutton Trust-EEF Teaching and Learning Toolkit*, https://educationendowmentfoundation.org.uk/pdf/generate/?u=https://educationendowmentfoundation.org.uk/pdf/toolkit/?id=132&t=Teaching%20and%20Learning%20Toolkit&e=132&s=

EEF (2018e), 'Magic Breakfast', https://educationendowmentfoundation.org.uk/projects-and-evaluation/projects/magic-breakfast/

EEF (2018f), 'Individualised instruction', *Sutton Trust-EEF Teaching and Learning Toolkit*, https://educationendowmentfoundation.org.uk/evidence-summaries/teaching-learning-toolkit/individualised-instruction/

EEF (2018g), 'Collaborative learning', *Sutton Trust-EEF Teaching and Learning Toolkit,* https://educationendowmentfoundation.org.uk/evidence-summaries/teaching-learning-toolkit/collaborative-learning/

EEF (2018h), 'Arts participation', *Sutton Trust-EEF Teaching and Learning Toolkit,* https://educationendowmentfoundation.org.uk/evidence-summaries/teaching-learning-toolkit/arts-participation/

EEF (2018i), 'Sutton Trust-EEF Teaching and Learning Toolkit and EEF Early Years Toolkit: Technical appendix and process manual'. London: EEF. https://educationendowmentfoundation.org.uk/public/files/Toolkit/Toolkit_Manual_2018.pdf

EEF (2019a), 'Promising projects', https://educationendowmentfoundation.org.uk/tools/promising/

EEF (2019b), 'Teensleep', https://educationendowmentfoundation.org.uk/projects-and-evaluation/projects/teensleep/

EEF (2019c), 'Glasses in Classes', https://educationendowmentfoundation.org.uk/projects-and-evaluation/projects/glasses-in-classes/

EEF (2019d), 'Healthy Minds', https://educationendowmentfoundation.org.uk/projects-and-evaluation/projects/developing-healthy-minds-in-teenagers/

Farrow, S., Tymms, P. and Henderson, B. (1999), 'Homework and attainment in primary schools', *British Educational Research Journal*, 25, (3), 323–341.

Forgeard, M., Winner, E., Norton, A. and Schlaug, G. (2008), 'Practicing a musical instrument in childhood is associated with enhanced verbal ability and nonverbal reasoning', *PloS One*, 3, (10), e3566.

Gamoran, A. (1992), 'Synthesis of research: Is ability grouping equitable?', *Educational Leadership*, 50, (2), 11–17, www.indiana.edu/~pcl/rgoldsto/courses/dunloskyimprovinglearning.pdf

Geake, J. (2008), 'Neuromythologies in education', *Educational Research*, 50, (2), 123–133.

Gielen, S., Tops, L., Dochy, F., Onghena, P. and Smeets, S. (2010), 'A comparative study of peer and teacher feedback and of various peer feedback forms in a secondary school writing curriculum', *British Educational Research Journal*, 36, (1), 143–162.

Gillies, R. M. (2016), 'Cooperative learning: Review of research and practice', *Australian Journal of Teacher Education*, 41, (3), 3.

Gladwell, M. (2009), *Outliers: The story of success*. London: Penguin.

Gladwell, M. (2014), *David and Goliath*. London: Penguin.

Gorard, S., See, B. H. and Davies, P. (2012), 'The impact of attitudes and aspirations on educational attainment and participation'. York: Joseph Rowntree Foundation. www.jrf.org.uk/sites/default/files/jrf/migrated/files/education-young-people-parents-full.pdf

Greenwood, P. M. and Parasuraman, R. (2016), 'The mechanisms of far transfer from cognitive training: Review and hypothesis', *Neuropsychology*, 30, (6), 742.

Gridley, H., Astbury, J., Sharples, J. and Aguirre, C. (2011), 'Benefits of group singing for community mental health and wellbeing'. Carlton: Victorian Health Promotion Foundation.

Guskey, T. R. and Jung, L. A. (2011), 'Response-to-intervention and mastery learning: Tracing roots and seeking common ground', *The Clearing House: A Journal of Educational Strategies, Issues and Ideas*, 84, (6), 249–255.

Guskey, T. R. and Pigott, T. D. (1988), 'Research on group-based mastery learning programs: A meta-analysis', *The Journal of Educational Research*, 81, (4), 197–216.

Gutman, L. M. and Schoon, I. (2013a), 'Essential life skills'. London: EEF. https://educationendowmentfoundation.org.uk/evidence-summaries/evidence-reviews/essential-life-skills/

Gutman, L. M. and Schoon, I. (2013b), 'The impact of non-cognitive skills on outcomes for young people. A literature review.' London: EEF/Cabinet Office.

Hallam, S. (2015), *The Power of Music: A research synthesis of the impact of actively making music on the intellectual, social and personal development of children and young people*. London: International Music Education Research Centre.

Hanushek, E. A. and Rivkin, S. G. (2010), 'Generalizations about using value-added measures of teacher quality', *American Economic Review*, 100, 267–271.

Harford, S. (2017), 'Ofsted's findings about the school curriculum', *Ofsted Blog*, https://educationinspection.blog.gov.uk/2017/10/11/ofsteds-findings-about-the-school-curriculum/

Hargreaves, E. (2011), 'Teachers' feedback to pupils: "Like so many bottles thrown out to sea?"', in: R. Berry and B. Adamson (eds.), *Assessment Reform in Education*. Dordrecht: Springer, pp. 121–133.

Harlen, W. and Deakin Crick, R. (2002), 'A systematic review of the impact of summative assessment and tests on students' motivation for learning', *Research Evidence in Education Library*, Issue 1. London: EPPI-Centre, Social Science Research Unit, Institute of Education.

Hattie, J. (2008), *Visible Learning: A synthesis of over 800 meta-analyses relating to achievement*. Abingdon: Routledge.

Hattie, J. and Timperley, H. (2007), 'The power of feedback', *Review of Educational Research*, 77, (1), 81–112.

Helsen, W. F., Baker, J., Schorer, J., Van Winckel, J. and Williams, M. A. (2013), 'The relative age effect in European Professional Soccer: Is there any difference after ten years of research?', *Journal of Exercise, Movement, and Sport*, 45, (1).

Herold, B. (2017), 'The case(s) against personalized learning', *Education Week*, http://stimuli.no/sites/default/files/u19/Personalized_Learning.pdf

Higgins, S. (2018), *Improving Learning: Meta-analysis of intervention research in education*. Cambridge: Cambridge University Press.

Higgins, S. and Hall, E. (2004), 'Picking the strawberries out of the jam: Thinking critically about systematic reviews and meta-analysis', *British Research Association Conference. September 2004 Manchester Metropolitan University*.

Higgins, S., Kokotsaki, D. and Coe, R. (2011), 'Toolkit of strategies to improve learning: Summary for schools spending the Pupil Premium'. London: Sutton Trust. www.cem.org/attachments/1toolkit-summary-final-r-2-.pdf

Higgins, S., Xiao, Z. and Katsipataki, M. (2012), 'The impact of digital technology on learning: A summary for the Education Endowment Foundation'. London: EEF. https://educationendowmentfoundation.org.uk/evidence-summaries/evidence-reviews/digital-technology/

Hill, H. C., Rowan, B., and Ball, D. L. (2005), 'Effects of teachers' mathematical knowledge for teaching on student achievement', *American Educational Research Journal*, 42, (2), 371–406.

Hollingsworth, J. R. and Ybarra, S. E. (2017), *Explicit Direct Instruction (EDI): The power of the well-crafted, well-taught lesson*. Thousand Oaks, CA: Corwin Teaching Essential.

Horak, V. M. (1981), 'A meta-analysis of research findings on individualized instruction in mathematics', *Journal of Educational Research*, 74, (4), 249–253.

Howard-Jones, P. A. (2014), 'Neuroscience and education: myths and messages', *Nature Reviews Neuroscience*, 15, 817–824.

Independent Teacher Workload Review Group (2016), 'Eliminating unnecessary workload around marking', https://assets.publishing.service.gov.uk/government/uploads/system/uploads/attachment_data/file/511256/Eliminating-unnecessary-workload-around-marking.pdf

Jackson, J. (2011), 'FA plans change for young talent to overcome the relative age effect', *Guardian*, www.theguardian.com/football/2011/jun/19/fa-plans-age-group-football

Jerrim, J., Austerberry, H., Crisan, C., Ingold, A., Morgan, C., Pratt, D., Smith, C. and Wiggins, M. (2015), 'Mathematics mastery: Secondary evaluation report'. London: EEF. https://educationendowmentfoundation.org.uk/public/files/Projects/Evaluation_Reports/EEF_Project_Report_Mathematics_Mastery_Secondary

Kingston, N. and Nash, B. (2011), 'Formative assessment: A meta-analysis and a call for research', *Educational Measurement: Issues and Practice*, 30, (4), 28–37.

Kirby, P. (2016), 'Shadow schooling: Private tuition and social mobility in the UK'. London: Sutton Trust. www.suttontrust.com/wp-content/uploads/2016/09/Shadow-Schooling-formatted-report_FINAL.pdf

Kirschner, P. A., Sweller, J. and Clark, R. E. (2006), 'Why minimal guidance during instruction does not work: An analysis of the failure of constructivist, discovery, problem-based, experiential, and inquiry-based teaching', *Educational*

Psychologist, 41, (2), 75–86, www.cogtech.usc.edu/publications/kirschner_Sweller_Clark.pdf

Klein, P. D. (2003), 'Rethinking the multiplicity of cognitive resources and curricular representations: Alternatives to "learning styles" and "multiple intelligences"', *Journal of Curriculum Studies*, 35, (1), 45–81.

Kyriakides, L., Creemers, B. P. and Charalambous, E. (2018), 'Searching for differential teacher and school effectiveness in terms of student socioeconomic status and gender: Implications for promoting equity', *School Effectiveness and School Improvement*, 30, (3), 286–302.

Lee, B. K., Patall, E. A., Cawthon, S. W. and Steingut, R. R. (2015), 'The effect of drama-based pedagogy on pre K–16 outcomes: A meta-analysis of research from 1985 to 2012', *Review of Educational Research*, 85, (1), 3–49.

Leung, K. C. (2018), 'An updated meta-analysis on the effect of peer tutoring on tutors' achievement', *School Psychology International*, 40, (2), 200–214.

Littleton, K. and Mercer, N. (2013), *Interthinking: Putting talk to work*. Abingdon: Routledge.

Lloyd, C., Edovald, T., Kiss, Z., Skipp, A., Morris, S. and Ahmed, H. (2015a), 'Paired reading: Evaluation report and executive summary'. London: EEF.

Lloyd, C., Edovald, T., Kiss, Z., Skipp, A., Morris, S. and Ahmed, H. (2015b), 'Durham Shared Maths Project: Evaluation report and executive summary'. London: EEF.

Lortie-Forgues, H. and Inglis, M. (2019), 'Most rigorous large-scale educational RCTs are uninformative: Should we be concerned?', *Educational Researcher*, in press.

Ma, X., Zhou, Z., Yi, H., Pang, X., Shi, Y., Chen, Q., Meltzer, M. E., le Cessie, S., He, M., Rozelle, S. et al. (2014), 'Effect of providing free glasses on children's educational outcomes in China: Cluster randomized controlled trial', *British Medical Journal*, 349:g5740.

Major, L. E. (2012), 'What really improves children's learning?', *Guardian*, www.theguardian.com/teacher-network/2012/feb/02/children-learning-sutton-trust-feedback

Major, L. E. and Machin, S. (2018), *Social Mobility and Its Enemies*. London: Pelican Books.

McKee, G., Sims, K. R. and Rivkin, S. G. (2015), 'Disruption, learning, and the heterogeneous benefits of smaller classes', *Empirical Economics*, 48, (3), 1267–1286.

Meissel, K., Parr, J. M. and Timperley, H. S. (2016), 'Can professional development of teachers reduce disparity in student achievement?' *Teaching and Teacher Education*, 58, 163–173.

Mercer, N. (2002), *Words and Minds: How we use language to think together*. Abingdon: Routledge.

Moats, L. C. (1998), 'Teaching decoding', *American Educator*, 22, (1), 42–49.

Montessori, M. (1939), *The Erdkinder and the Functions of the University*. Amsterdam: Association Montessori Internationale.

Mowry, T. (2007), Interview for *Seventeen*, 19 November, www.seventeen.com/celebrity/interviews/a1164/tia-wiw17-1207/

Muller, J. Z. (2018), *The Tyranny of Metrics*. Princeton, NJ: Princeton University Press.

Murphy, R., Weinhardt, F., Wyness, G. and Rolfe, H. (2017), 'Lesson Study: Evaluation report and executive summary'. London: EEF. https://educationendowmentfoundation.org.uk/public/files/Projects/Evaluation_Reports/Lesson_Study.pdf

Murphy, P. K., Wilkinson, I. A., Soter, A. O., Hennessey, M. N. and Alexander, J. F. (2009), 'Examining the effects of classroom discussion on students' comprehension of text: A meta-analysis', *Journal of Educational Psychology*, 101, (3), 740.

Murtagh, L. (2014), 'The motivational paradox of feedback: Teacher and student perceptions', *Curriculum Journal*, 25, (4), 516–541.

Musch, J. and Hay, R. (1999), 'The relative age effect in soccer: Cross-cultural evidence for a systematic discrimination against children born late in the competition year', *Sociology of Sport Journal*, 16, (1), 54–64.

Musk, E. (2012), Interviewed by Lance Ulanoff for *Mashable*, 13 April, https://mashable.com/2012/04/13/elon-musk-secrets-of-effectiveness/?europe=true

NHS (2018), 'Physical activity guidelines for children and young people', www.nhs.uk/live-well/exercise/physical-activity-guidelines-children-and-young-people/

Nilson, L. B. (2013), *Creating Self-Regulated Learners: Strategies to strengthen students' self-awareness and learning skills*. Sterling, VA: Stylus Publishing.

Nuthall, G. (2007), *The Hidden Lives of Learners*. Wellington: NZCER Press.

Nye, B., Hedges, L. V. and Konstantopoulos, S. (2002), 'Do low-achieving students benefit more from small classes? Evidence from the Tennessee class size experiment', *Educational Evaluation and Policy Analysis*, 24, (3), 201–217.

Ofsted (2009), 'An evaluation of National Strategy intervention programmes', https://dera.ioe.ac.uk/326/1/An%20evaluation%20of%20National%20Strategy%20intervention%20programmes.pdf

Ofsted (2019), 'Ofsted launches a consultation on proposals for changes to the education inspection framework', www.gov.uk/government/news/ofsted-launches-a-consultation-on-proposals-for-changes-to-the-education-inspection-framework

Pashler, H., McDaniel, M., Rohrer, D. and Bjork, R. (2008), 'Learning styles: Concepts and evidence', *Psychological Science in the Public Interest*, 9, (3), 105–119.

Perraudin, F. (2018), 'Thousands of teachers caught cheating to improve exam results', *Guardian*, www.theguardian.com/education/2018/feb/11/thousands-of-teachers-caught-cheating-to-boost-exam-results

Public Health England (2014), 'The link between pupil health and wellbeing and attainment', https://assets.publishing.service.gov.uk/government/uploads/system/uploads/attachment_data/file/370686/HT_briefing_layoutvFINALvii.pdf

Puzio, K. and Colby, G. T. (2013), 'Cooperative learning and literacy: A meta-analytic review', *Journal of Research on Educational Effectiveness*, 6, (4), 339–360.

Riener, C. R. and Willingham, D. T. (2010), 'The myth of learning styles', *Change: The Magazine of Higher Learning*, 42, (5), 32–35.

Romero, C. C. (2009), 'Cooperative learning instruction and science achievement for secondary and early post-secondary students: A systematic review', PhD thesis, Colorado State University, ProQuest Dissertations Publishing: 3374617.

Rowling, J. K. (1998), *Harry Potter and the Chamber of Secrets*. London: Bloomsbury.

Roy, P., Styles, B., Walker, M., Morrison, J., Nelson, J. and Kettlewell, K. (2018), 'Best practice in grouping students: Intervention A: Best practice in setting: Evaluation report and executive summary'. London: EEF. https://educationendowmentfoundation.org.uk/public/files/Projects/Evaluation_Reports/Intervention_A_-_Best_Practice_in_Setting.pdf

Rubie-Davies, C. M., Blatchford, P., Webster, R., Koutsoubou, M. and Bassett, P. (2010), 'Enhancing learning? A comparison of teacher and teaching assistant interactions with pupils', *School Effectiveness and School Improvement*, 21, (4), 429–449.

Samuels, S. J. (2007), 'The DIBELS tests: Is speed of barking at print what we mean by reading fluency?', *Reading Research Quarterly*, 42, (4), 563–566.

Schucan-Bird, K., Tripney, J. and Newman, M. (2013), 'The educational impacts of young people's participation in organised sport: A systematic review', *Journal of Children's Services*, 8, (4), 264–275.

Secker, J., Spandler, H., Hacking, S., Kent, L. and Shenton, J. (2007), 'Art for mental health's sake', *Mental Health Today*, Jul-Aug, 34–36.

Sharples, J., Webster, R. and Blatchford, P. (2018), 'Making best use of teaching assistants: Guidance report'. London: EEF. https://educationendowmentfoundation.org.uk/tools/guidance-reports/making-best-use-of-teaching-assistants

Shulman, L. (2004), *The Wisdom of Practice: Essays on teaching, learning and learning to teach*. San Francisco, CA: Jossey-Bass.

Sibieta, L., Kotecha, M. and Skipp, A. (2016), *Nuffield Early Language Intervention: Evaluation report and executive summary*. London: Education Endowment Foundation.

Simpson, A. (2017), 'The misdirection of public policy: Comparing and combining standardised effect', *Journal of Education Policy*, 32, (4), 450–466.

Singh, A., Uijtdewilligen, L., Twisk, J. W., Van Mechelen, W. and Chinapaw, M. J. (2012), 'Physical activity and performance at school: A systematic review of the literature including a methodological quality assessment', *Archives of Pediatrics & Adolescent Medicine*, 166, (1), 49–55.

Skinner, B. F. (1938), *The Behavior of Organisms: An experimental analysis*. New York: BF Skinner Foundation.

Slavin, R. E., Hurley, E. A. and Chamberlain, A. (2003), 'Cooperative learning and achievement: Theory and research', in I. B. Weiner (ed.), *Handbook of Psychology*. Hoboken, NJ: John Wiley and Sons, pp. 177–198.

Smith, E. and Gorard, S. (2005), '"They don't give us our marks": The role of formative feedback in student progress', *Assessment in Education: Principles, Policy and Practice*, 12, (1), 21–38.

Smith, H. and Higgins, S. (2006), 'Opening classroom interaction: The importance of feedback', *Cambridge Journal of Education*, 36, (4), 485–502.

Sobel, H. S., Cepeda, N. J. and Kapler, I. V. (2011), 'Spacing effects in real-world classroom vocabulary learning', *Applied Cognitive Psychology*, 25, (5), 763–767.

Standley, J. M. (2008), 'Does music instruction help children learn to read? Evidence of a meta-analysis', *Update: Applications of Research in Music Education*, 27, (1), 17–32.

Stanovich, K. E. (1986), 'Matthew effects in reading: Some consequences of individual differences in the acquisition of literacy', *Reading Research Quarterly*, 21, (4), 360–407.

Steenbergen-Hu, S. and Cooper, H. (2013), 'A meta-analysis of the effectiveness of intelligent tutoring systems on K–12 students' mathematical learning', *Journal of Educational Psychology*, 105, (4), 970.

Stockard, J., Wood, T. W., Coughlin, C. and Rasplica Khoury, C. (2018), 'The effectiveness of direct instruction curricula: A meta-analysis of a half century of research', *Review of Educational Research*, 88, (4), 479–507.

Strathern M. (1997), '"Improving ratings": audit in the British University system', *European Review*, 5, (3), 305–321.

Sutton Trust (2005), 'Rates of eligibility for free school meals at the top state schools', www.suttontrust.com/wp-content/uploads/2005/06/1RatesOfEligibilityforFreeSchoolMealsattheTopStateSchools.pdf

Sutton Trust (2011), 'Improving the impact of teachers on pupil achievement in the UK – interim findings', www.suttontrust.com/wp-content/uploads/2011/09/2teachers-impact-report-final.pdf

Sutton Trust (2013), 'NFER poll results on teachers spending pupil premium', www.suttontrust.com/newsarchive/nfer-poll-results-teachers-spending-pupil-premium/

Syed, M. (2011), 'Born supremacy that needs to be challenged', *The Times*, www.thetimes.co.uk/article/born-supremacy-that-needs-to-be-challenged-sdkphbdkbgn

Sykes, E., Bell, J. and Rodeiro, C. (2009), *Birthdate Effects: A review of the literature from 1990-on*. Cambridge: Cambridge Assessment. www.

cambridgeassessment.org.uk/images/109784-birthdate-effects-a-review-of-the-literature-from-1990-on.pdf

Sylvester, R. and Thomson, A. (2018), 'Schools excluding difficult pupils to keep grades up', *The Times*, www.thetimes.co.uk/article/schools-exclude-troublesome-pupils-to-keep-grades-up-r3sqw9wxv

Teaching Times (2018), 'GCSE Curriculum Narrowing Under EBacc', www.teachingtimes.com/news/gcsecurriculum.htm

Thurston, A. and Cockerill, M. (2017), *Peer Tutoring in Schools* (5th edn.). Belfast: Queen's University Belfast. https://pure.qub.ac.uk/portal/files/130755742/PairedReadingManual_v5.doc

Timperley, H. (2008), 'Teacher professional learning and development', in J. Brophy (ed.), *The Educational Practices Series – 18*. Brussels: International Academy of Education and International Bureau of Education. http://edu.aru.ac.th/childedu/images/PDF/benjamaporn/EdPractices_18.pdf

Timperley, H., Wilson, A., Barrar, H. and Fung, I. (2007), *Teacher Professional Learning and Development*. Auckland: Ministry of Education. www.oecd.org/education/school/48727127.pdf

Tolmie, A. K., Topping, K. J., Christie, D., Donaldson, C., Howe, C., Jessiman, E., Livingstone, K. and Thurston, A. (2010), 'Social effects of collaborative learning in primary schools', *Learning and Instruction*, 20, (3), 177–191.

Torgerson, C., Brooks, G., Gascoine, L. and Higgins, S. (2019), 'Phonics: reading policy and the evidence of effectiveness from a systematic "tertiary" review', *Research Papers in Education*, 34, (2), 208–238.

Trudeau, F. and Shephard, R. J. (2008), 'Physical education, school physical activity, school sports and academic performance', *International Journal of Behavioral Nutrition and Physical Activity*, 5, (1), 10.

Vaag Iversen, J. M. and Bonesrønning, H. (2013), 'Disadvantaged students in the early grades: Will smaller classes help them?', *Education Economics*, 21, (4), 305–324.

Van der Kleij, F. M., Feskens, R. C. and Eggen, T. J. (2015), 'Effects of feedback in a computer-based learning environment on students' learning outcomes: A meta-analysis', *Review of Educational Research*, 85, (4), 475–511.

Vaughan, R. (2015), 'UK among world's worst for "teaching to the test"', research finds', *TES*, www.tes.com/news/uk-among-worlds-worst-teaching-test-research-finds

Watson, A. and Kelso, G. L. (2014), 'The effect of Brain Gym® on academic engagement for children with developmental disabilities', *International Journal of Special Education*, 29, (2), https://pdfs.semanticscholar.org/8f82/69575e9471324fe0fa38d26a3920c063045b.pdf

Webster, R., Blatchford, P., Bassett, P., Brown, P., Martin, C. and Russell, A. (2010), 'Double standards and first principles: Framing teaching assistant support for pupils with special educational needs', *European Journal of Special Needs Education*, 25, (4), 319–336.

Wiliam, D. (2006), *Excellence in Assessment: Assessment for learning*. Cambridge: Cambridge Assessment. www.assessnet.org.uk/e-learning/file.php/1/Resources/Excellence_in_Assessment/Excellence_in_Assessment_-_Issue_1.pdf

Wiliam, D. (2011), 'What is assessment for learning?', *Studies in Educational Evaluation*, 37, (1), 3–14.

Wiliam, D. (2015), 'The research delusion', *TES*, www.tes.com/news/research-delusion-0

Willingham, D. T., Hughes, E. M. and Dobolyi, D. G. (2015), 'The scientific status of learning styles theories', *Teaching of Psychology*, 42, (3), 266–271.

Wilsdon, J., Allen, L., Belfiore, E., Campbell, P., Curry, S., Hill, S., Jones, R., Kain, R., Kerridge, S., Thelwall, M., Tinkler, J., Viney, I., Wouters, P., Hill, J. and Johnson, B. (2015), 'The metric tide: Report of the independent review of the role of metrics in research assessment and management', https://responsiblemetrics.org/wp-content/uploads/2019/02/2015_metrictide.pdf

Worth, J., Sizmur, J., Walker, M., Bradshaw, S. and Styles, B. (2017), 'Teacher observation: Evaluation report and executive summary'. London: EEF. https://educationendowmentfoundation.org.uk/public/files/Projects/Evaluation_Reports/Teacher_Observation.pdf

Yeh, S. S. (2010), 'Understanding and addressing the achievement gap through individualized instruction and formative assessment', *Assessment in Education: Principles, Policy & Practice*, 17, (2), 169–182.

Yorke, H. (2017), 'Government orders investigation into public school cheating scandal as regulator considers change in rules', *Telegraph*, www.telegraph.co.uk/education/2017/08/31/government-orders-investigation-public-school-cheating-scandal/

INDEX

Index